BOUGHT AND SOLD
FOR ENGLISH GOLD?

Bought and Sold for English Gold?

EXPLAINING THE UNION OF 1707

Christopher A. Whatley

TUCKWELL PRESS

First published in Great Britain in 2001 by
Tuckwell Press
The Mill House
Phantassie
East Linton
East Lothian EH40 3DG
Scotland

First edition 1994
Second edition © Christopher A. Whatley 2001

ISBN 1 86232 140 X

The Publishers acknowledge subsidy from
the Scottish Arts Council towards the
publication of this volume

British Library Cataloguing in Publication Data
A catalogue record for this book is available on
request from the British Library

The right of Christopher A. Whatley to be identified as
the author of this work has been asserted by
him in accordance with the
Copyright, Design and Patent Act 1988

Typeset by Antony Gray
Printed and bound by Creative Print and Design
Ebbw Vale, Wales

CONTENTS

ACKNOWLEDGEMENTS

The author is indebted to Professor T. C. Smout of the University of St Andrews for his encouragement and continued interest in this project. Professor Allan I. Macinnes of the University of Aberdeen generously provided information. Sydney Wood of the Northern College kindly commented on an earlier draft. Senior students at both St Andrews and Dundee universities helped to clarify my thinking on the subject. Professor R. H. Campbell has been a patient, helpful and gently-critical editor. Mrs Sara Reid ably and efficiently transformed a poorly-typed script into one ready for use by the printer.

C. A. W
Dundee, March 1994

PREFACE TO 2ND EDITION

I am grateful to John and Val Tuckwell of Tuckwell Press for giving me the opportunity to refine and develop my ideas on the subject of the Union of 1707 and, by re-publishing *Bought and Sold*, making it available once more to students, teachers and academics, as well as to a wider public. My understanding of the topic has been deepened through the study of primary documents I had not seen prior to the publication of the first edition. My thanks are due to staff at the National Archives of Scotland, particularly David Brown, and to Jane Anderson, the Archivist at Blair Castle. All have provided me with invaluable assistance and support. So too has Steve Connelly of Perth and Kinross Archives. I have also had the opportunity to reflect upon and incorporate the new work of scholars who have written on the Union and related issues during the past decade. I am also indebted to Mrs Sara Reid, of the Department of History, University of Dundee, for her work on preparing the text for the printers. Her copy-editing skills are of immense value to me and many of my departmental colleagues.

The publishers wanted to make this edition more reader-friendly than the first, and in keeping with the format adopted for the 'Scottish History Matters' series of which this title is one, intrusive source references have been removed from the text and confined to a shorter list of essential endnotes for each chapter. A Select Bibliography enables readers to follow up aspects of the topic in greater depth. The additional Appendices make for a much more comprehensive publication.

For their help in securing the illustrations and granting permission for them to be used I should like to express my gratitude to His Grace the Duke of Hamilton, Dr Rosalind K. Marshall, formerly of the Scottish National Portrait Gallery, and George Dalgleish of the National Museums of Scotland.

C. A. W.
Dundee, April 2001

LIST OF PLATES

1. *Downsitting of the Scottish Estates (Parliament), c. 1680*

2. *Royal review of the British Fleet, c. 1708*

3. *Queen Anne (1665–1714)*

4. *Sir James Douglas, 2nd Duke of Queensberry (1662–1711)*

5. *Sir John Clerk of Penicuik (1676–1755)*

6. *Anne, Duchess of Hamilton (1632–1716)*

7. *Lord Bellhaven's speech in Parliament, 2 November 1706*

8. *Signatories to the Articles of Union, 2 July 1706*

9. *Standard English quart wine measure, Stirling, 1 May 1707*

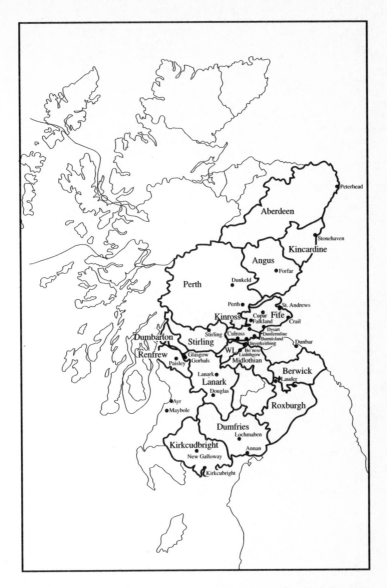

Counties and burghs which sent addresses against the proposed union to the Parliament in Edinburgh in 1706. In addition, many parishes petitioned against, with particularly sizeable clusters around Hamilton in Lanarkshire, and in Lowland Perthshire. Pro-union petitions, such as one which was sent from Montrose in Angus, were rare.

INTRODUCTION

In July 1999, in Edinburgh, the first Scottish Parliament to be assembled since 1707 was formally opened by Her Majesty, Queen Elizabeth. Its 129 newly elected members – females as well as males – were obviously proud of their roles as actors on the stage of Scotland's history, re-convening the country's ancient Parliament. At this early stage, they basked in the warm glow of (largely passive) public approval. This momentous step, prepared for through the work of the cross-party Constitutional Convention in the first half of the 1990s, had been set in motion by the result of the Referendum in September 1997, with the electorate voting three to one in favour of devolution and somewhat less firmly for a Parliament with tax-raising powers. Buoyed by the strength of the popular vote, the new 'New Labour' government – only elected to office in May 1997 – produced the Scotland Bill in December.

This was in stark contrast to the situation in the early months of 1707, as the last session of the Parliament in an independent Scotland was adjourned (on 25 March 1707), and preparations were made to transfer its powers to Westminster. Less than two years beforehand Scotland and England had been at loggerheads, with Scots residing in England on the verge of being declared aliens. Scotland's main exports to England were to be excluded. In the intervening period English troops had been moved close to the Scottish border.

No evidence of a Scottish fanfare to mark the occasion has come to light; on the contrary, public opinion was overwhelmingly hostile. Indeed during the final stages of the all-male discussions on the Articles of the Union in the Scottish Parliament there were well-founded rumours that an armed rising was being organised in Lanarkshire. The angry crowds which had turned out in Edinburgh and some other Scottish towns in the autumn of 1706 to express their opposition to the proposed incorporating union – by burning the

Articles in Glasgow, Stirling and Dumfries for example – had dispersed, but only temporarily. In February 1707 both Her Majesty's Commissioner, the Duke of Queensberry, and the Lord Chancellor, the Earl of Seafield – along with other members of Scotland's nobility – declined to assemble at the Cross in Edinburgh as they had traditionally done to celebrate the monarch's birthday.[1] Queen Anne, like her predecessor King William, had been an active proponent of union between the two countries, and had pushed hard for incorporation. Afraid of the growling mob, Scotland's political leaders would only appear in public if the magistrates could maintain order, and line the streets with soldiers. It was in England that Queensberry, an ardent pro-unionist, had been applauded as he rode south in April. On 1 May, the day of the Union's inauguration, Queen Anne was the focal point of a procession to the thanksgiving service in St Paul's Cathedral and the subsequent triumphal celebrations which engulfed London. Medallions were struck to commemorate the Union, and a new Union flag was designed. Queen Anne's wisdom and foresight were the subject of laudatory addresses, such as that which prefaced John Chamberlayne's *Magna Britannia Notitia: Or, The Present State of Great Britain, With divers Remarks on the Ancient State thereof,* published in 1708. Britons had become acutely aware of the dangers of the French threat to the two disputatious kingdoms:

> What Methods he might possibly take, in case of a Separation, we foresaw; but how to prevent the Consequences of those Methods, We knew not. One way We knew would effectually remove our Fears, and that was to Incorporate both Kingdoms into One. But at this Juncture was rather to be wish'd than hop'd for. The Ancient Difficulties still remain'd, and New ones were sprung up, which were equally forbidding; and the Mischiefs attending such a Separation appear'd every Day more terrible. Under these Difficulties your Majesty reliev'd Us, and, by Your unparalell'd Prudence in the Choice of proper Agents, and your unweary'd Industry in urging them on to complete the Work, it was in short time brought to a happy Conclusion.

Sentiments of this sort were rarely expressed in Scotland. On 1 May 1707, most Scottish burghs, as far as is known, were quiet, and business went on as usual. Yet even at this early date, suspicions abounded about the motives of those Scottish parliamentarians who had voted in favour of the Union. It is almost certainly the case that the air 'A Parcel o' Rogues in a Nation' dates back to this period. So too does the assertion that Scotland had been 'bought and sold for English gold' , a phrase which is now usually identified with Robert Burns.[2] The arrival of twelve horse-drawn waggons bearing the bullion and exchequer bills which represented the Equivalent (the 'Price of Scotland', see below, Chapter 2), was greeted in Edinburgh by a mob contemptuous of the arrival of 'Judas money', and who went 'along the streets curseing the very English nation'. The frenzied Anglophobia which had resulted in the seizure and subsequent execution in Leith by the Edinburgh mob of Captain Green and some crew members of his ship the *Worcester* had not simply evaporated. During the summer of 1707 Lord Stormont reported from the Borders that there had been a 'Solemne battle' between 36 Scottish and 53 English fishermen during which some Englishmen had been severely wounded: 'the quarrell', he declared, 'was nationall'.[3]

Within weeks of its inauguration, active opposition to the Union began to be seen, heard and felt. It is important to emphasise this point: there is a school of thought which, somewhat mysteriously (perhaps because they wish to play down the impact of the Union in Scotland's modern history ?), confidently asserts that for most Scots, the effects of the working out of the Union in Scotland were inconsequential. In fact, during the first two or three decades after 1707 popular resentment as the union settlement was implemented was widespread. Even in the mid-1720s, Daniel Defoe was struck during a tour of Scotland by the coldness of the welcome he and his party encountered in the east of Scotland. This was explained not by the quelling of the Jacobite Rising of 1715 or the defeat of the Spanish incursion of 1719, but by the effects of the Union. Only in the west, and in particular Glasgow, were the short-term effects of the Union viewed as beneficial. Glasgow was the exception, even in 1708, when the extent of discontent was so great elsewhere that government agents and advisers were convinced that if French troops landed on Scottish soil, there would be a popular Jacobite rising.[4]

By far the most common complaint was the appearance in Scotland of what one contemporary described as 'Shoalls' of customs and excise officers, whose posting was designed to improve the efficiency of revenue collection north of the border. It was anticipated that Scottish state revenues, no more than £110,000 per annum in the 1700s, and less than had been collected in the 1650s, would rise with the Union to £160,000.[5] Attacks on such officers of the state were not new in 1707, but they were much more frequent, as not only were state officials more numerous and more rigorous in carrying out their duties, but the Articles of Union had also specified additional targets for taxation. These included salt, the single, virtually indispensable, commodity which brought virtually every Scottish household into the market. Salt officers, appointed to watch the steaming salt pans, were also detested in and around the salt-making communities, where individuals went to considerable lengths to evade payment of the salt tax.[6] The bans which the Scottish Parliament had placed on some Irish commodities prior to 1707 (such as cattle, oats and oatmeal, and butter), became more effective from 1707, leading in Port Glasgow for example to rioting and the violent freeing from prison of Gavin Pow, a 'merchant traveller' who had formerly traded across the Irish Sea. Such crowd action, in effect a form of protest against 'the operation of laws tending to the supply of food', was not confined to the west.[7] Early in August 1707 the Duke of Atholl was informed that the brewers in Edinburgh had stopped working and raised a mob to 'put out ye fires of others'. The cause was given as 'the Severity of the Gadgers [excisemen]'.[8] This was in a city where – in the short run – circulating capital was diminishing rapidly: late in October 1707 Alexander Areskine wrote that few of his acquaintances were left, 'a great many were gone and goeing to London', and 'takeing a great Deall of money with them'.[9]

During the first half of the eighteenth century assaults on the royal warehouses and customs and excise officers in Scotland became endemic, and so severe that troops were frequently called in to support them. Lives were lost (a minimum number – 60 – has only been crudely calculated and is almost certainly an underestimate) as panicking soldiers shot at rampaging mobs, while officers who were unfortunate enough to be captured by a crowd were invariably beaten, bruised and bloodied.[10] While the involvement of the labouring poor in incidents of this sort almost certainly had an economic motivation in that they received small payments from the smuggling gangs for their assistance, contemporaries were convinced that other factors were also at work. These included anger about the Union and its effect on some trades; dislike of the officers sent north – the 'very scum and canalia of the country', according to George Lockhart of Carnwath; and a belief that the tax revenue collected in Scotland was being remitted to England.[11]

Yet for almost three centuries Scotland has been ruled from Westminster, which post-devolution continues to hold considerable reserve powers: over foreign policy, national security, macro-economic policy, employment law, trade, and social security, along with matters such as broadcasting, abortion law and gambling.

Until the 1970s most Scottish electors appear to have accepted the fact that their Members of Parliament represented their interests in London rather than Edinburgh. Post-Union, a highly lucrative system of Westminster patronage eventually softened most discontent felt amongst the political classes and their beneficiaries. Ordinary Scots began to feel the benefits of the English connection from the middle of the eighteenth century, as employment opportunities increased, in part the result of energetic campaigning in London on behalf of Scottish interests.[12] Yet a strand of Scottish patriotism not only survived but also manifested itself strongly – as in the numbers of copies of Blind Harry's *Wallace* circulating in the eighteenth century, the ubiquity of the sound of the words and tune of 'Scots Wha Hae' in west-central Scotland during the period of the Radical War, the formation of the National Association for the Vindication of Scottish Rights in the 1850s and construction of the remarkable Wallace Monument (completed 1869) near Stirling. The last two instances owed much to the Unionist-Nationalism of the middle decades of the nineteenth century, during which Scots sought more from the Union, not less unionism.[13] This co-existed with a powerful sense of Britishness and commitment to the Empire and a United Kingdom which had fought, and was judged by many to have won, moral as well as military victories in two world wars in the twentieth century. From the end of the nineteenth century there were periodic demands within and outside Westminster for Home Rule, although these were invariably short-lived or weak or divided. The first, marshalled by the Scottish Home Rule Association, formed in 1886, was devolutionist and democratic rather than separatist in intention. Pressures for independence, however, born of a growing awareness that the benefits of union were less obvious in the post-industrial era, and articulated by an increasingly buoyant Scottish National Party, persuaded the established parties that it would be electorally prudent to offer some measure of devolution to the Scots, although that meted out in media-sized bites by the Conservative and Unionist Party led in Scotland by Michael Forsyth, Secretary of State from 1995, did not include constitutional change, on the grounds that this would imperil the Union.

Thus far there has been a reluctance to sever completely the umbilical cord which unites the Scots with England, Wales and Northern Ireland. There are those who argue that to cut the ties more deeply would result in the loss of substantial economic nourishment for Scotland.[14] Others believe that a united Britain is greater than the sum of its parts. The Duke of Queensberry's conviction in 1707 that 'posterity will reap the benefit of the union of the two kingdoms' still has its adherents, although in diminishing numbers on both sides of the Border.

The reasons for the Union of 1707 have long been hotly debated, and although numerous historians have laboured hard on the subject, the degree of disagreement among them can still be considerable. One reason for this is that it is an exceedingly difficult puzzle to unravel. Another is that many of those who have engaged in the debate have deep personal convictions about the Union and the English connection, as unionists, nationalists or patriots, sometimes consciously, sometimes not. Analysis of the personal and educational background of nineteenth-century historians of the Union, and the intellectual climate in which they worked, does much to explain their attachment to the Union, as well as what initially seems to be a contradiction (hinted at above): a patriotism which operated on both a symbolic and linguistic level, alongside a belief that Scottish interests were best served within some sort of union framework.[15]

Not all historians are persuaded that the Union was a significant event, and argue that it had a slighter impact on subsequent Scottish development than has been suggested in some quarters, including my own recent book, *Scottish Society 1707–1830: Beyond Jacobitism, towards industrialisation*. Nevertheless, the Act of Union has become a major and enduring landmark in Scottish history, which 'casts a long shadow . . . both backwards and forwards'.[16] And whatever actually happened as a result of it, there can be no denying its symbolic and mythical significance for Scottish politics and culture. It is an icon which flits in and out of the weave of Scottish literature – in much of the Jacobite poetry of the eighteenth century for instance, including that of Robert Burns as well as his predecessor Robert Fergusson, who declared powerfully in 'The Ghaists', that:

> Black be the day that e'er to England's ground
> Scotland was eiket by the Union's bond.

Partly because of contemporary concerns about Scotland's place within the British political system – even now, with the first phase of devolution having taken place – the Union is still very much a live issue. Contemporaries were even more likely to be partisan, yet it is upon their written evidence that historians depend so heavily, thus making it difficult to judge who is telling the truth. A prime example is Daniel Defoe, better known as a novelist and journalist, but who also wrote extensively on the Union, including a *History* of it not long after 1707. In one sense he was in a good position to do so, as he was located in and around Edinburgh for some fifteen months from September 1706. His writings, including letters sent to London reporting in detail and with considerable authority on events in Scotland both before May 1707 and immediately afterwards, are thus invaluable sources. Yet Defoe, a defender of Protestantism and vocal opponent of Louis XIV of France's imperial and trading ambitions, was in Scotland as a paid agent, a spy and propagandist (in which role he had had some modest success in England in the early 1700s) of the English government, and must therefore be read with considerable caution. To his credit, however, he openly admitted that the Union was unpopular in Scotland and, notwithstanding his own efforts to calm Scottish fears, recognised the dangers that a people so incensed by it posed for Westminster and Queen Anne.

On the other, anti-union side, was George Lockhart of Carnwath, estate proprietor and early agricultural improver and also a member of both the Scottish Parliament (1703–1707) and later (1708–14) the British Parliament. Throughout his adult life he was also a Jacobite. He was arrested for his part in the Rising of 1715 but unlike his brother, Philip, who was court-marshalled and shot, he was later released – and resumed his pro-Jacobite activities. Between 1708 and 1711 Lockhart penned his *Memoirs Concerning the Affairs of Scotland* which, when they first appeared in print in 1714, brought to light information which had hitherto been widely suspected but unproven: that several members of the Scottish Parliament had received secret payments in return for their support for the Court-led incorporating union. Lockhart's *Memoirs*, considered treasonable when they first appeared, articulated in print a condemnation which has become deeply ingrained in the Scottish public's consciousness, through song, poetry, the media and the writings of not a few historians, and represents perhaps a desire to remove any semblance of legitimacy from a political arrangement with which Scots have rarely been entirely comfortable.

Lockhart was also blessed with an acidic turn of phrase and provided penetrating and sometimes withering sketches of his political contemporaries, whose identities, although part-concealed, were not hard to decipher. Anti-unionists, then and now, find enormous pleasure in Lockhart's description of the Earl of Stair as 'the Origine and Principal Instrument of all the Misfortunes, that befell either the King or Kingdom of Scotland', or the description of the rise to prominence of the 'Proud, Arrogant, Greedy [and] extreamly False' Earl of Glasgow (who distributed the £20,000 sent to Scotland from the Treasury, on the orders of Queen Anne, for payment to those MPs who 'might prove humorous and ungovernable'), an instance of how far 'the Height of Ambition and Impudence, without any Merit, will bring a Man in this World'. Indeed so telling was this source, and damaging to the cause of those historians who attempted to justify the Union, that it has been alleged that publication of a further edition between that of 1817 and the most recent in 1995 was 'suppressed by tacit censorship'.[17] Although this charge ignores the question of whether there was a market for source material which was readily available to interested scholars in the main libraries and may even reveal a case of acute nationalist paranoia, there is no doubt that Lockhart's *Memoirs* provide us with telling first-hand information on the events surrounding the Union. But even if the account Lockhart provides is accurate, allowance must be made both for the writer's pungent style of writing, and for the fact that a man of his political persuasion can hardly have been expected to produce a rounded discussion of the topic.

In fact, that he found Lockhart's *Memoirs* so 'silly' and misleading on the causes of Union, was one of the motives given by Sir John Clerk of Penicuik for compiling his own *History*, which has only recently been translated from the Latin in which it was originally written. Clerk's account is an important one. A member of the Scottish Parliament from 1703 and one of the union commissioners, Clerk was another witness to the events in and around Parliament which preceded the Union of 1707. Nevertheless, even though Clerk was active for the Union cause, it is known that as a new parliamentarian, he had been impressed by Andrew Fletcher's speeches on the Act of Security of 1703, and some commentators have doubted the sincerity of his defence of the Union. The suggestion has been made that his *History* was an attempt on Clerk's part to justify his role in 1705 and 1706, when his political advancement had depended upon the patronage of the High Commissioner the Duke of Argyll, the Earl of Stair and the Duke of Queensberry. Conscious of the strength of feeling in Scotland against the proposed union, he had only accepted nomination as one of the union commissioners as Queensberry had threatened to withdraw his 'friendship', although all the indications currently available show that Clerk did not stint in his service to the Crown.[18]

Bias in sources, and their incompleteness, and how to deal with these problems, present critical philosophical and methodological difficulties for most historians, and raise questions about the limits of historical knowledge. The Union debate provides a prime example of the importance for both history students and their teachers of knowing the context, purpose and motive of all writers, be they contemporaries or historians. A. J. Youngson has argued, with telling effect, that when historians are confronted with conflicting evidence and of necessity have to select, 'to prefer one interpretation . . . to another', they will select and prefer 'so as to produce a version of events which . . . [the historian] . . . finds believable and agreeable – agreeable in the sense that it accords with his view of human nature and how things are apt to happen'.[19] The present writer cannot be sure that he should be entirely exempted from such charges, although every attempt will be made to peer beyond what blinkers may obscure his judgement. As will be seen, there have been contributors to the debate who have almost certainly deliberately eschewed such intellectual self-discipline, with the result that their error-strewn accounts have followed tortuously illogical paths to their pre-ordained conclusions. Unacknowledged political partisanship is something of a hindrance if the goal is to offer a mature understanding of the Scottish past.

The primary aim of this book is to make some sense of the controversies which surround the Union, and identify and assess the various arguments which have been developed to explain why it happened. Readers who are unfamiliar with the background to 1707 or the chronology of events, or with the chief personalities and political groupings, should consult one of the standard narrative accounts, of which there are a number, two of the best being by MacKinnon (1896) and Daiches (1977), although both are now out of print. Also hard to find, outside the better libraries, is G. S. Pryde's short but succinct survey (1950), which has the advantage of containing a full transcript of the Articles of Union. More recently these – an invaluable historical source in their own right, and too rarely consulted – were reprinted in Volume 5 of the *Modern Scottish History* series of books edited by Cooke, Donnachie, MacSween and Whatley (1998), and they are reprinted here as well. The broader context of Union is dealt with in books which cover longer periods of Scottish history, such as Mitchison (1983), Lynch (1991) or Brown (1992). Fine readable studies of the Union itself are available. William Ferguson's *Scotland's Relations with England: A Survey to 1707* (1977, 1994) is a classic and P. H. Scott's *Andrew Fletcher and the Treaty of Union* (1992) is lively. Both, however, are highly-coloured by the nationalist persuasions of their authors. In Scott's case this may have caused him to overlook key evidence which, if considered, would necessarily alter his conclusions.

Although this book has been written by an author trained as an economic and social historian, it incorporates the work of political as well as intellectual historians, the intention being to produce a multi-dimensional study. Indeed one of the less productive features of the debate about the causes of the Union has been the tendency for historians to split into camps determined partly by their scholarly predilections. Most notable is the divide between political and economic interpretations, the former tending to take the short view while the latter generally adopts a longer time-frame. The intellectual history of the Union often seems one step removed from what was happening on the ground, yet the views of thinking Scots on the fundamental question of what was the best course of action for their nation's future mattered then as they do now. It is self-evident that such a failure of historical dialogue does nothing to advance our understanding of the causes of Union. The thrust of the argument which follows is that there were many factors at work in the making of Union, none of them the sole property of any single historical sub-grouping.

The book is arranged as follows. Immediately after this Introduction is a chapter which provides background information on the Union and identifies some of the key issues in the debate. Following this are two chapters which attempt to clarify the debate about causes and reach some tentative conclusions. These chapters will also attempt to show how interpretations have changed over time. The final chapter provides a synthesis, and offers a brief, up-to-date explanation for the Union of 1707.

But a word of warning is required. For ease of understanding, the material in Chapters 2 and 3 is presented under a series of individual sub-headings, some of which broadly represent either a particular school of thought, or a prominent strand from a complicated argument. It should be stressed that this way of proceeding can have the effect of over-simplifying the views of those historians whose work is referred to. In fact most of them advance a number of interrelated reasons in their explanations for the Union. Monocausal explanations are rare and usually entirely inadequate. In order to do justice to the historians whose work is referred to and grasp fully the richness of their arguments, and indeed judge the validity of the evidence upon which these have been constructed, readers must both engage in a process of cross-referencing, and, where possible, read the texts referred to in full.

The principal source has been the wealth of secondary literature which continues to flow out in book, article and chapter form. Use has also been made of some primary sources, and these are referred to directly in this book. Some benefit can be derived from an examination of examples of primary material. To this end a small number of contemporary documents has been transcribed to form a series of Appendices. These will enable readers to observe for themselves something of the nature of the evidence. The documents too can be used as a focus for discussion in tutorials and seminars.

The response of readers to the first, 1994, edition of this short book was, overall, highly gratifying. Not all those who read it were convinced by the arguments, however. One critic even suggested that they had 'more to do with propaganda than scholarship', and represented a return to an old and discredited orthodoxy, that is with Union resulting from a fair exchange of free trade for the Scots in return for the surrender of their Parliament.[20] This is not quite what I argued. The same critic, who, somewhat remarkably, called upon the poems and songs of Robert Burns in order to sustain his argument for the importance of bribery and corruption in passing the Union, accused me of distorting the evidence, misrepresentation, confusion and failing to appreciate the political realities of the time.[21] This new, revised and expanded version of *Bought and Sold for English Gold?* examines and assesses some of the criticisms of the first edition, not least because of their public nature and the fact that the subject of the Union – and Scotland's relations with England – is one which is of importance outside the portals of the universities. Regrettably, as has been hinted already, there are views on the subject being published for public consumption, which are at best over-simplified and at worst deeply misleading. We have an historiography of the Union which is scarred by bias and has led to respectable voices in Scottish society concurring in the belief that the Union was 'a masterpiece of bribery and corruption'.[22] This helps to generate an inferiorist view of Scotland's history, as a nation which was helplessly manipulated by England in England's interest, and played little part in determining its own destiny.

Equally importantly, especially for student readers, the new edition of this book also incorporates much of the new material on the subject which has been published since 1994. While the conclusions reached in the current edition are not very different from those of 1994, fresh findings and further reflection have produced some modifications. Greater emphasis, for example, will be paid to the wider European context in which the British union occurred. More work from those historians whose commitment is to the history of the four kingdoms, England, Scotland, Wales and Ireland, has become available. Unfortunately, however – and nothing pejorative is intended – some English historians have failed to search out and draw upon the more recent detailed research which has been conducted north of the Border, the effect of which is to produce somewhat dated or tired analyses of the causes of the Union of 1707. During the 1990s, however, historians from all corners of Britain and Ireland have made significant strides forward in unpicking the complex interplay of factors which bound the four nations together and intersected their distinctive histories, albeit that the ties have been loosening since the Irish Free State was established in 1922.[23]

As has been implied, the opportunity too has been taken to explore more of the voluminous primary records which have survived from the period. Contrary to the assertions of some of the more self-righteous critics, however, who are not averse to boasting about their familiarity with the sources, these do not provide 'overwhelming evidence' that English bullying and bribery provide the sole explanation for the parliamentary union with England. This is only part of the story. The reasons for union were much more interesting than that. This was so throughout early-modern Europe, when the number of independent polities was almost halved between the early sixteenth century and the end of the eighteenth century. Rarely, however, can the creation of a new composite state be satisfactorily accounted for simply by reference on one side to the ambitions of a strong ruler, and on the other to a puny and powerless victim.[24]

The conclusions in the final chapter of this book will provide little succour for those who seek guidance for the future through the lessons of the past. The conditions which prevailed in the early 1700s are no longer present. On the other hand, many of the

considerations which weighed heavily in the minds of those responsible for leading Scotland towards Union in 1707 are the same:
what does being Scottish mean; where does Scotland stand on the
monarchy; what is Scotland's relationship with Europe, including
Scandinavia, to be; how significant is the English connection;
where do Scotland's best economic interests lie; and is national
independence worth having, whatever the cost?

NOTES TO INTRODUCTION

1. Blair Castle, Atholl MSS, (7), 10, Patrick Scott to the Duke of Atholl, 8 February 1707.

2. C. A. Whatley, 'Burns and the Union of 1707', in K. G. Simpson (ed), *Love & Liberty. Robert Burns: A Bicentenary Celebration* (East Linton, 1997), 183–5.

3. Blair Castle, Atholl MSS, (7), 80, Lord Stormont to the Duke of Atholl, 11 August 1707.

4. J. S. Gibson, *Playing the Scottish Card: The Franco-Jacobite Invasion of 1708* (Edinburgh, 1988), 101–3.

5. J. Goodare, *State and Society in Early Modern Scotland* (Oxford, 1999), 321–2.

6. C. A. Whatley, *The Scottish Salt Industry, 1570–1850: An Economic and Social History* (Aberdeen, 1987), 1–2, 116–20; C. A. Whatley, 'How tame were the Scottish Lowlanders during the Eighteenth century?', in T. M. Devine (ed.), *Conflict and Stability in Scottish Society, 1700–1850* (Edinburgh, 1990), 5–7.

7. W. Hector, *Selections from the Judicial Records of Renfrewshire* (Paisley, 1876), 67–8.

8. Blair Castle, Atholl MSS, (7), 82, Patrick Scott to the Duke of Atholl, 5 August 1707.

9. Ibid., (7), 189, Alexander Areskine to the Duke of Atholl, 29 October 1707.

10. Whatley, 'How tame were the Scottish Lowlanders?', 20.

11. Anon., *Some Considerations On the Present State of Scotland in a Letter to the Commissioners and Trustees for Improving the Fisheries and Manufactures* (1744), 5–6.

12. C. A. Whatley, *Scottish Society: Beyond Jacobitism, towards industrialisation* (Manchester, 2000), 99–116.

13. G. Morton, *Unionist Nationalism: Governing Urban Scotland, 1830–1860* (East Linton, 1999).

14. See C. H. Lee, *Scotland and the United Kingdom: the economy and the union in the twentieth century* (Manchester, 1995).

15. See the interesting thesis by Kino Iwazumi, 'The Union of 1707

in Scottish Historiography', (unpublished MPhil, University of St Andrews, 1996).

16. B. Lenman, 'Union, Jacobitism and Enlightenment', in R. Mitchison (ed), *Why Scottish History Matters?* (Edinburgh, 1991), 48.

17. P. H. Scott, in his Foreward to D. Szechi (ed.), *'Scotland's Ruine': Lockhart of Carnwath's Memoirs of the Union* (Aberdeen, 1995), vii.

18. See D. Duncan (ed.), Sir John Clerk, *History of the Union of Scotland and England* (Edinburgh, 1993), 1–29.

19. A. J. Youngson, *The Prince and the Pretender: A Study in the Writing of History* (London, 1985), 13.

20. P. H. Scott, *The Herald*, 4 March 1995.

21. P. H. Scott, Review: 'The Truth about the Union', *Scottish Affairs*, 11 (Spring 1995), 52–9.

22. Sir Alastair Dunnet, former Editor of *The Scotsman*, in *The Herald*, 13 September 1996.

23. Three very different examples are B. Bradshaw and J. Morrill (eds.), *The British Problem, c.1534–1707: State Formation in the Atlantic Archipelago* (London, 1996); D. L. Smith, *A History of the Modern British Isles, 1603–1707: The Double Crown* (London, 1998), and S. J. Connolly (ed.), *Kingdoms United? Great Britain and Ireland since 1590: Integration and Diversity* (Dublin, 1999). The volumes by Bradshaw and Morrill, and Smith, contain extensive bibliographies.

24. M. Greengrass (ed.), *Conquest and Coalescence: The Shaping of the State in Early Modern Europe* (London, 1991), viii, 1.

I

The Background

On 1 May 1707 Scotland ceased to have its own parliament, and legislative authority passed to Westminster. The process of formal integration had begun earlier, with the Union of the Crowns in 1603. Informal integration and moves towards a greater Britain had been taking place for much longer. The step taken in 1707, which created a unitary British state, was therefore not unprecedented. Edward I had attempted to rule Scotland along colonial lines for a short period from the late 1290s. The 'Rough Wooing' of 1544–50 represented another attempt on the part of England to rule Scotland, and indeed it was during this time that the term 'Great Britain' was first used on any scale. James VI had persuaded both of his parliaments to set up commissions to treat for a limited form of union, more secure than a mere dynastic union and, although this came to nothing, he was able to control the Scottish Parliament through his management and appointment of the members of the Lords of the Articles, and with the judicious use of the Convention of the Estates, whose legislative powers were limited. He also extended his hold over his territories by policing the Borders, initiating plantation in Ulster and engaging in a 'military and legislative offensive' in the Gaelic north-west of Scotland. By formally annexing Orkney and Shetland, James not only extended and secured his frontier in the north, but also consolidated Britain's territorial waters.[1] In 1650–1 Oliver Cromwell succeeded in invading and conquering Scotland, and imposed a short-lived political union, notable for its insensitivity to Scots' aspirations, with a single British Parliament. Scottish interest in a commercial confederation with England was revived in 1664, and again in 1668, but soon foundered upon English fears of the Scots' competitive strength in the carrying trade, along with concerns amongst the coal and salt interests of the north-east of England about the potential damage which would result from Scottish competition.

After the Restoration, with Charles II on the throne, John Maitland, Duke of Lauderdale, Secretary of State for Scotland between 1661 and 1680, also pushed for and succeeded in getting negotiations started for an incorporating union, although with only lukewarm support in Scotland. Within weeks of the Commissioners from both Parliaments meeting, the proposals were dropped (although broadly, the Articles of Union of 1707 were based upon them), following Lauderdale's demand for equal representation for the Scots in the joint parliament.[2] Both at the beginning and the end of his reign, William of Orange advocated incorporation between his two bickering subject nations, although his ministers had little enthusiasm for such a step. Under Anne too, who succeeded to the throne in March 1702, negotiations for an incorporating union – pressed for hard by the new monarch – took place, but broke down on the issues of taxation and compensation for the Scots.[3]

Union, then, was a recurring theme in Anglo-Scottish relations during the seventeenth century, especially as Scots, 'unenthusiastic, but realistic', in the words of John Morrill, sought to give the regal union 'institutional coherence'. There were other factors at work too, which made closer union between the two countries more likely. Composite or dynastic unions of formerly autonomous states – the new nation states – were commonplace phenomena in early-modern Europe, the age of the 'universal monarchy', where a single prince ruled over an extensive territory aided by a sizeable army of government officials. By the time of Queen Anne's death in 1714, the number of bureaucrats serving the British state was 10,000, six times more than in the 1630s. But the multiple or composite monarchy was not unusual either, where monarchs were torn between the demands of more than one subject nation or state.[4] From the 1620s new developments in political thinking emerged, with pre-emptive defence and legitimate conquest, 'yielding an approach to union more aggressive than . . . hitherto'.[5] In tandem there was posited the rival concept of confederations of states, 'represented as antagonistic to extensive territorial empire'. Within either of these frameworks the British union looks much less anomalous than it does when examined solely in parochial Scottish or even British terms, and can reasonably be described as 'a thoroughly European event'. Indeed as early as

1605 Sir Thomas Craig advocated an incorporating, imperial union between the two kingdoms as a measure which would be as 'formidable as *Hispanicum Imperium* [the Spanish empire] itself'. Between the fourteenth century and the end of the eighteenth century, the number of independent polities in Europe is estimated to have fallen from around 1,000 to 350. New states were being formed from territories which in the past had been divided by ruling families, inheritance and war. Larger, more efficient state bureaucracies were necessary to raise the funds to pay for the new permanent armies and navies which nations had to create in order to survive in an era of territorial expansion and militant mercantilism. Expanding states jostled with each other to carve out great economic empires and to defend jealously guarded trading routes. One example was Russia, centralised by mid-century, which, in order to develop as a naval and maritime power, sought access thereafter to the sea, first by reaching the Black Sea and then, during the Great Northern War (1700–21) with Sweden under Charles XII, the Baltic. As French power under Louis XIV grew, so did pressures for closer unification in the Spanish and Austrian monarchies and the United Provinces, as well as in Britain. The invasion of the Netherlands by Louis XIV in 1672 focused English attention on the fearful threat posed by French ambition to England's emergent empire of the seas, although the argument that hostility to Popery provided some fuel for English Francophobia should not be ruled out entirely. The restored Stadholder, William of Orange, also recognised the danger to his own country and Europe of French aggrandisement, and began to prepare for the struggle over the Spanish Succession which looked likely to follow the death of Charles II, the remaining Spanish Habsburg. It is notable that between 1707 and 1716, the Austrian, Spanish and British states were re-ordered, albeit in different ways. What emerges from a survey of the relations between the European states is that from the English perspective at the turn of the eighteenth century, union with Scotland would stiffen England's defence against French ambitions of universal monarchy, as well as help bolster the British imperial adventure overseas.

The two nations had much in common and, notwithstanding their differences, there were several areas of convergence and even integration. They had been moving more closely together since around 1560 when Scotland's traditional alliance with Catholic France was severed and the Scots, much influenced by John Knox, gravitated instead towards Protestant England. Both countries rejected Roman Catholicism and in their distinctive ways were ardent exponents of a Protestant culture which united them in a common cause from the reign of Queen Elizabeth onwards. The 'Glorious Revolution', the flight into exile of James VII and the subsequent arrival of William of Orange as monarch of the two nations was confirmation in both of their commitment to the 'true religion', and of a shared animosity towards France and the ambitions of Louis XIV to create a Counter-Reformation Catholic empire in western Europe.[6] Anti-Catholicism was widespread on both sides of the border. Almanacs in Scotland – 50,000 were reputedly sold annually in Aberdeen alone in the 1680s – were as militantly Protestant as their English counterparts.[7] After 1670 union proposals excluded religious union, although ecclesiastical politics were very much to the fore during the debates which preceded the 1707 Union. By the 1690s moderatism was softening older animosities in both countries and allowed for religious pluralism, making it more likely that a British civil union might accommodate more than one religious establishment. This was unlike most other unitary states or composite monarchies of the period, which were uniconfessional. Episcopalian ministers were purged in Scotland after 1690 for their failure to endorse the Williamite regime, not on the grounds of their faith. William himself had been prepared to accept a Presbyterian establishment, but not kirk-led extremism. Religious denomination mattered less than it had in the early seventeenth century, provided of course that however small the sect, it was within the Protestant camp. The road to religious diversity within a political union was by no means even, however, as will be seen, and the staunchly Presbyterian Scottish Covenanters would have no truck with a people whose episcopalian national church was error-ridden, sinful and potentially malignant, likely to divert those Scots sworn to reform worship in England from their contract with God. Indeed there are grounds for arguing that the religious issue sponsored divergence rather than convergence.[8] On the other hand, and often overlooked, British union, on Scottish terms, had been a serious option for those Scottish ideologues who sought through the covenant and confederalism to impose a constitutional settlement involving God, king and people in the three kingdoms which would secure the position of the true Reformed Church.[9]

With the removal of the royal court from Edinburgh to London in 1603, a rapid process of anglicisation is thought to have occurred, certainly at the level of the political elite. Increasingly, Scots statesmen, devoting their services to a London-based monarch, were playing to an English audience as, in effect, British politicians. Indeed some, led by the rising house of Argyll, preferred to describe themselves as North Britons rather than Scots. Later, George Mackenzie, Earl of Cromartie, declared that he had 'lost faith in the viability of Scottish nationhood', and wished to see their replacement by 'Brittains', 'our true, our honorable denomination'. Increasingly too, English was the commonly understood language outside the Gaelic-speaking parts of Scotland. Even there, aristocratic chiefs and some of their womenfolk were adopting the speech, writing styles and values of the metropolis, whence they acquired fashionable clothes and consumer goods. Lower down the social scale, too, Gaelic was less often the sole language of a people who were increasingly anglophone.[10] New research into Scots' attendance at universities such as Leiden in the Netherlands, the teaching there and their reading matter, has revealed the extent to which they shared with their English counterparts an interest in European learning and ideas.[11]

There were other forces at work too, which, on the face of it, were pulling together the inhabitants of the British island of the Atlantic archipelago. Above all there was the single monarchy, which by the early 1700s had been in place for a century. Centralising ambitions on the part of the royal court had even begun to have their impact on the culture and politics of the Hebridean periphery, through measures such as the Statutes of Iona (1609) and their successors.[12]

Over time, the nature of state building on both sides of the Border was another factor which indicates congruity, and later, would make it easier to effect a parliamentary union. In both countries, the Parliaments had risen in status and authority, and were the source of legal statutes. (Mark Goldie has argued that this is unlikely to have drawn the two institutions together, so significant were the differences between them. Not the least of these was the greater hold the monarchy had over the Scottish Parliament, even after 1689. The 18th Article of Union recognised that the two countries' legal systems differed.) After 1625 the fiscal power of the Scottish state increased, and as in England its mainstay was customs and excise, supplemented after 1678 and 1690 by revived land taxes. Tax collection methods in Scotland, however, were much less effective after the Restoration, and resort was had to fresh but ultimately disappointing sources of revenue, the hearth tax of 1690, and three poll taxes, in 1693, 1695 and 1698. By the eve of the Union there were English counties which were paying more tax than the whole of Scotland. The ratio between the tax yields of the two countries was 10.5 to 1 in 1659 but by the time of the negotiations over parliamentary union, had widened to 36 to 1.[13]

In the 1640s, a modern, well-equipped Scottish army was created under the Covenanters. Although small – better described in later decades as a 'home-defence force' – compared to its English counterpart, and comprising between only 2–3,000 men, by the end of the seventeenth century, both English and Scottish armies were under the command of a single, British, monarch. Increasingly, army commissions were in the gift of the English ministry. Scottish soldiers too were recruited into the English army, although such regiments maintained their Scots identity as the Scots Greys and the Royal Scots.

This is not to suggest, however, that the Union of 1707 was inevitable. At the political level convergence still had a long way to go. Close inspection reveals that rather few Scots were members of the royal households of either Charles II or William III. Queen Anne's Court, according to Keith Brown, 'was dominated by English Tory families and the Scottish presence was reduced to two doctors', but anyway power was shifting away from Court towards Parliament. Opportunities for Court service were reduced by around one-third between the reigns of Charles I and Anne. In the House of Commons between 1660 and 1690 there were only 13 Scots peers or their sons, and these were mainly Englishmen or anglicised Scots. The two countries continued to have separate Privy Councils and, by and

large, separate honours systems. With the restoration of the Order of
the Thistle in 1687, the monarch was able to reward Scots, but
outside the English system of honours. No Scots, for example, were
made Knights of the Bath. There are indications too that the Scottish
nobility spent less time in London than is often assumed, and tended
to rent rather than purchase property in the capital.[14] It is worth
noting that such was the demand for portraits amongst the Scottish
political classes, in Scotland, that Brussels-born Sir John Medina was
persuaded to venture north in 1694, and performed the near-
monopolistic role which Sir Godfrey Kneller, principal painter to
William III from 1691, did in English aristocratic circles.[15]

Similarly, while it would be foolish to deny the impact of 'anglo-
phile, aristocratic and courtly' energies in Restoration Scotland,
Scots 'played a minimal role as either patrons of or contributors to
court culture'.[16] There was a strong attachment to Scottish cultural
forms and productions, and to imported European ideas, fashions
and architectural styles – as indeed there was in England. Scottish
painting, the decorative nature of which in the reign of James VI
was distinctively Scottish, owed much to French and, later, Dutch
influences. But Scottish cultural achievement flowed outwards too.
Although English painters worked in Scotland, Scots worked furth of
Scotland. Ham House, the English residence of the Duke of
Lauderdale, was designed by the Scottish architect Sir William Bruce
and became 'the greatest Scottish house in England'.[17] In music, too,
Scottish airs and songs were heard and appreciated south of the
Border, while the Aberdeen-born John Abell sang and composed in
royal circles. Scottish patriotism found its musical form in John
Clerk's cantata *Leo Scotiae Irritatus* (The Scottish Lion Angered),
composed during the Scots' unsuccessful attempt to establish a
colony at Darien.[18] It has been forcibly argued that several of the
antecedents of the Enlightenment in eighteenth-century Scotland
can be found in the intellectual and cultural innovations of the later
seventeenth century.

As will be seen later, one of the most powerful pressures which
appeared to be driving Scotland closer towards England was economic. But there were alternatives to a 'union of trade' with England,
or at least these were sought. The bitter experience and searing

memory of the Cromwellian union of 1654 had led to fears about absorption by England, as well as the prospect that England would impose a union by force. One possibility was joint trading ventures. Establishing workable commercial agreements with the English was no easy matter. In the early 1630s, for example, a Scottish-led attempt, supported by Charles I, to set up a British fishery was unsuccessful partly because of Scottish objections to Englishmen fishing off the Western Isles.[19] Another was to construct a Scottish colonial empire. Within a year of the collapse of union negotiations in November 1670, Lauderdale began to pursue colonial ambitions on behalf of Scotland, and although these came to nothing, just over a decade later James VII warranted Scottish colonies in South Carolina (1682) and East New Jersey (1685). And after the rude awakening from the Darien dream in 1700, and as England drove the Scots to the negotiating table with the Aliens Act in 1705, the Scottish Parliament looked once more to the potential of the fisheries to lift the country out of its economic malaise.

Nor should it necessarily be assumed that incorporation and the loss of Scottish independence were the result of a long-held desire on the part of the English for union with Scotland. This was a course of action which had previously been considered only during periods of crisis. The much-used demonological concept of 'English' hegemonic ambition towards Scotland fails to acknowledge the fact that after 1688–89 there were significant policy differences between the emergent Whig and Tory parties. Thus in July 1706, after the Commissioners from both countries had settled the broad terms of union, the Whig First Lord of the Treasury, Lord Godolphin, reported to the Duke of Marlborough that if the proposals were approved in the Scottish Parliament, the 'angry party [the Tories]' would oppose them at Westminster.[20] The point will be developed further later. The Scots were more often regarded as a nuisance, to be ignored if possible. In March 1708 John Chamberlayne admitted as much in the preface to his *Present State of Great-Britain*, remarking that not only did he have little first-hand knowledge of Scotland but that few 'even of our [England's] most Inquisitive Men, have a just Idea of the Condition of that Country', with 'many Parts of Africa and the Indies' being better known 'than a Region which is contiguous to our own'.

Nevertheless, what events such as the Glencoe massacre and the Darien disaster showed was that in order to co-exist peaceably, the two countries had to have some sort of understanding with each other. As has been seen, various proposals for union – mainly on the part of Scots – were made during the seventeenth century. Regal union might have provided the basis for a solution, and indeed this arrangement seemed likely to continue, although in an amended form. By the early 1700s, however, tensions within the regal union were making it both unpopular and unworkable, and more radical constitutional schemes were proposed. The boldest of these was advocated by Andrew Fletcher of Saltoun, who outlined a plan for a confederal union, with a more independent Scottish Parliament, equal in power to its English counterpart. In turn, this British confederation would become part of a new political division of Europe, on the basis of sovereign cities and their surrounding territories.[21]

Nevertheless, all previous proposals for further union, including those in the recent past (1668, 1670 and 1689), had foundered. Relations between the two countries have been described by Michael Lynch as cold, sour and acrimonious, and the unstable chemistry between them had periodically exploded into open warfare. Indeed, it has been argued that far from converging, the two countries had been drifting further apart between 1688 and 1707, as Scottish aversion to English domination grew. Ironically, this, and the fact that the Scots looked as though they were developing an independent foreign policy, forced England to look beyond regal union and towards an incorporating union.

The Claim of Right of the Convention of the Estates of 1689 not only condemned James VII's abuses of his power and replaced Episcopalianism with Presbyterianism, but also established the right of the moribund Scottish Parliament to be called regularly. In the following year the Lords of the Articles were abolished, thus removing a major arm of royal influence in Scotland, and transferring substantial powers to Parliament, even though legislation was still subject to royal veto. The monarch also continued to appoint the major officers of state. Nevertheless, the mechanisms for conflict between the monarch and the Parliament of Scotland were now in place, and were exploited by the latter ('acting with a vigour and independence which it had never shown before in all its long and not very splendid history'), as dissatisfaction with King William grew in Scotland.[22] This was in spite of the fact that in 1689 he had been warmly welcomed in Scotland, even by those who would later oppose him – as well as parliamentary union.

In the years immediately prior to 1707, then, relations between England and Scotland were at a distinctly low ebb. Two Acts passed by the Scottish Parliament in 1703, the Act of Security and the Act anent Peace and War, were contrary to English interests and also confident declarations of Scottish independence, and hardly seemed to herald voluntary moves on the part of the Scots towards closer links with England. Although there is some debate about what significance should be attached to the Wine and Wool Acts (passed in 1703 and 1704 respectively), they were at least irritating to the English, upon whose interests they would have an adverse impact, even though this may not have been their primary aim. Nor were English merchants particularly anxious to forge closer links with or open their doors to the penurious Scots, despite the efforts of monarchs from the time of James VI to join the two nations.

What may seem remarkable, then, from this perspective is not only that union was accomplished, but that the Union of 1707 was an *incorporating* union. It not only marked the end of the Scottish Parliament (and, theoretically, that of England too), but it also slashed the size of the 'political' nation. Prior to its dissolution in May 1707, the single-chamber Scottish Parliament had a total of 247 members, drawn from the nobility, the barons (or shire representatives) and the burgesses. From May 1707 Scotland was to be represented at Westminster by 16 elected peers, and 45 MPs, 30 of whom were to represent the counties, 15 the burghs. It was assumed in Scotland that there would be a separate Privy Council in Edinburgh, and indeed this was secured by a clause in Article XIX of the Treaty of Union. Nevertheless, the Privy Council was abolished in 1708.

Paul Scott has argued that the distinction between a 'union' or a closer relationship between the two countries in some sort of federal arrangement, and incorporating union, whereby Scotland gave up its Parliament and therefore the ability to legislate separately on Scottish matters, is crucial. The potential benefits of the former had long been widely recognised in Scotland, and an ambitious variant had been sought by the Scots Covenanters between 1637 and 1651. Even in the months before the final passage of the Act of Union through the Scottish Parliament there were many who continued to favour union with England, but who were implacably opposed to incorporating union. This option, however, seen by James VI as the logical next step following the Union of the Crowns, and urged by King William and his successor Queen Anne (although supported with much less enthusiasm by English parliamentarians, the Tories in particular), carried with it far greater risks as far as Scotland was concerned. That regal union, without adequate checks on monarchs who tended to conflate national interest with English interest (despite James VI's initial efforts on the part of his fellow Scots), was not working to Scotland's advantage, became increasingly obvious as the aforementioned disenchantment with King William grew. The problem was clearly recognised by 1703, when a new Parliament was elected for the first time since 1689, and passed the uncompromisingly nationalistic Acts referred to above. But incorporating union was the only constitutional form which England would accept.[23] The Court's proposals for union were put by the English commissioners to their Scottish counterparts, at the Cockpit in London, on 16 April 1706. After three months of negotiations, much of which took the form of shadow boxing, the treaty was completed, subject to ratification by the two Parliaments. If it looked in the Scottish Parliament as though the opposition might succeed in defeating the Court proposals for 'an entire' union, Queen Anne had issued instructions that there was to be an adjournment.[24] By January 1707 the full treaty had been voted on and touched with the royal sceptre. On 25 March 1707 the Lord Chancellor, Queensberry, concluded the final session of the Scottish Parliament with a declaration of faith in Scotland's future within the united kingdom.

The Act of Union comprised twenty-five separate Articles, which covered all manner of subjects, from the appearance of the new nation's flag (Article I), through the succession to the crown (Article II), to matters of trade, taxes and finance (Articles IV–XVIII). These were often detailed and concerned with the needs of particularly influential pressure groups. The most significant of these was the landowners, some of whom obtained additional support from the Union through protection of their private rights which had been granted by the Scottish Privy Council. The legal system (Article XIX) and parliamentary representation (Articles XXII and XXIII) were also settled. The Treaty, however, did not result in complete incorporation (largely because of Scottish insistence that it should not), and several Scottish institutions retained their separate identity, the most important of these being the legal system, the royal burghs, the Church of Scotland (which was secured through a separate 'Act for securing the Protestant Religion and Presbyterian Church Government within the Kingdom of Scotland'), and the education system. Nor was political integration ever complete: throughout the eighteenth century and even beyond the 1832 Reform Act, which effectively brought the system of political 'management' to an end, Scotland managed with varying degrees of success to maintain a 'semi-independent' status within the new framework.[25]

NOTES TO CHAPTER I

1. A. I. Macinnes, 'Politically Reactionary Brits?: The Promotion of Anglo-Scottish Union, 1603–1707', in S. J. Connolly (ed.), *Kingdoms United? Great Britain and Ireland since 1500: Integration and Diversity* (Dublin, 1999), 44.
2. Ibid.., 50–2.
3. W. Ferguson, *Scotland's Relations With England: A Survey to 1707* (Edinburgh, 1994 ed), 198–203.
4. J. Morrill, 'The British problem, *c*.1534–1707', in B. Bradshaw and J. Morrill (eds.), *The British Problem, c.1534–1707: State Formation in the Atlantic Archipelago* (Basingstoke, 1996).
5. J. Robertson, 'Empire and union: two concepts of the early modern European political order', in J. Robertson (ed.), *A Union For Empire: Political Thought and the Union of 1707* (Cambridge, 1995), 5.
6. C. Kidd, 'Religious realignment between the Restoration and Union', in Robertson, *A Union for Empire*, 146.

7. L. Colley, *Britons: Forging the Nation, 1707–1837* (New Haven and London, 1992), 20.

8. M. Goldie, 'Divergence and Union: Scotland and England, 1660–1707', in Bradshaw and Morrill, *The British Problem*, 222–5.

9. Macinnes, 'Politically Reactionary Brits ?', 46–50.

10. D. U. Stiubhart, 'Women and gender in the Early Modern Gaidhealtachd', in E. Ewan and M. Meikle (eds.), *Women in Scotland, c.1100–c.1750* (East Linton, 1999), 242–3.

11. R. L. Emerson, 'Scottish cultural change 1660–1710 and the Union of 1707', in Robertson, *A Union for Empire*, 121–44.

12. A. I. Macinnes, *Clanship, Commerce and the House of Stuart, 1603–1788* (East Linton, 1996), 65–71.

13. Goodare, *State and Society in Early Modern Scotland* (Oxford, 1999), 321.

14. See K. Brown, 'The origins of a British aristocracy: integration and its limitations before the treaty of Union', in S. G. Ellis and S. Barber (eds.), *Conquest & Union: Fashioning a British State* (London, 1995), 222–49.

15. D. MacMillan, *Scottish Art, 1460–1990* (Edinburgh, 1990), 82; D. L. Smith, *A History of the Modern British Isles, 1603–1707* (London, 1998), 324.

16. H. Ouston, 'Cultural Life from the Restoration to the Union', in A. Hook (ed.), *The History of Scottish Literature, Volume 2: 1660–1800* (Aberdeen, 1988), 11.

17. MacMillan, *Scottish Art*, 77.

18. J. Purser, *Scotland's Music* (Edinburgh, 1992), 159–72.

19. B. Harris, 'Scotland's Herring Fisheries and the Prosperity of the Nation, c.1660–1760', *Scottish Historical Review*, LXXIX (April 2000), 44.

20. H. L. Snyder (ed.), *The Marlborough-Godolphin Correspondence* (3 vols., Oxford, 1975), II, 629.

21. For a recent, illuminating, contribution on Fletcher, see J. Robertson's Introduction to *Andrew Fletcher: Political Works* (Cambridge, 1997).

22. G. M. Trevelyan, *Ramillies and the Union with Scotland* (London, 1932), 179.

23. B. P. Levack, *The Formation of the British State* (Oxford, 1987), 30, 216.
24. B. C. Brown (ed.), *The Letters and Diplomatic Instructions of Queen Anne* (London, 1935), 190–1.
25. See D. McCrone, *Understanding Scotland: The Sociology of a Stateless Nation* (London, 1992).

2

A Survey of Causes: Statesmanship, Political Management, Bribery and Party Advantage

Statesmanship

From the Victorian era until as recently as the 1960s most professional historians who wrote about the Union were agreed that it was a 'good thing', an act of considerable foresight and statesmanship. According to Professor Hume Brown, sometime Historiographer Royal for Scotland, it was apparent from the correspondence of the leading supporters of Union that they were 'profoundly convinced of its necessity in the interests of both kingdoms [i.e. England and Scotland]'.[1] G. M. Trevelyan was of a similar view in 1932, and indeed this was still a perfectly respectable standpoint in 1962 when George S. Pryde, then Professor of Scottish History and Literature at the University of Glasgow, could confidently declare that the Union, 'grounded on common sense and reached through fair and open bargaining, was one of the most statesmanlike transactions recorded in our history'.[2]

Not surprisingly, therefore, historians of this persuasion were impressed by the political skills and in some cases what they believed to be the genuine commitment of individual leading pro-Union politicians, although to be fair, it should be pointed out that an historian such as Trevelyan was prepared to concede that the opposition case was not without foundation. Old books need not be bad books, and some of them are very good indeed.

The Duke of Queensberry, the Queen's Commissioner in Scotland in the last crucial months of 1706, often described as one of the 'chief architects' of the Union, was praised for the 'masterly manner' in which he 'steered the Union through the stormy seas of parliamentary debate', as well as for his 'serenity of temper' and the 'inexhaustible patience, watchfulness, and tact with which he held together his heterogeneous party, outmanoeuvred his opponents, and anticipated their designs'.[3] John Dalrymple, 1st Earl of Stair, 'the most unpopular statesman of the day', largely owing to his involvement in the Glencoe massacre of 1692, was judged by the same writer to have been a tireless and public-spirited supporter of Union, even though 'no office or pension was ever bestowed upon him'. William Seton, younger, of Pitmeddden, MP, and prominent pro-Union pamphleteer, has also been applauded: 'Measured, compact and logical, his contributions to the debate were at once full of matter and inspired by a grave sense of the national issues at stake'.[4]

Views such as these form an integral part of what has been described as the Whiggish interpretation of Scottish history, and in outlook owe not a little to the views of Henry Thomas Buckle, and his belief in 'progress', which, in Scotland's case, had advanced greatly since 1707.[5] The pro-Union convictions of the historians referred to above were thus to a large extent grounded in hindsight and shaped by their interpretation of the advantages which Union had brought: Dicey and Rait, for example, argued that 'any fair-minded man' in the early nineteenth century would have seen that in the previous hundred years the Union had 'doubled the strength of Great Britain ... enabled the country to resist the power of Louis XIV, and to withstand the far greater genius and power of Napoleonic despotism'. Only two years before the publication in 1920 of their *Thoughts On the Union Between England and Scotland*, Great Britain and the British Empire had defeated Germany in the First World War. As was noted in the Introduction, at the heart of the Empire lay the Westminster Parliament.

The argument that both Scotland and England gained much from the Union, and that the Scots, conscious of this, eventually committed themselves to it with a vengeance, is a persuasive one, which has recently been powerfully re-stated.[6] Certainly not be overlooked is Scotland's considerable contribution to both Britain and the British Empire in the eighteenth and nineteenth centuries. What is more relevant here, however, is whether or not the most ardent proponents of Union, or their supporters in the Scottish Parliament, envisaged all of the benefits it allegedly brought. Was it the prospect of these that persuaded them to support it?

Political Management and Bribery

The arguments which have been outlined above have subsequently been subjected to a barrage of criticism. Not the least of the objections is the proposition that, far from being statesmanlike, a considerable number of the Scottish parliamentarians who supported Union did so because they were bribed, either by cash payment, the offer or granting of a sinecure, or the prospect of office. This is not a novel or new proposition. Some contemporaries took this view. Somewhat ironically, considering the behaviour of the Duke of Hamilton in the Scottish Parliament, Ann Hay, on behalf of the Duke's mother, the Duchess of Hamilton, wrote contemptuously of those who had 'their eyes blinded with a gift'.[7] Certainly the venality of the Scots nobility appears to have shocked even the pro-Union propagandist Daniel Defoe, who wrote in April 1707 (after the Act of Union had been ratified, but before it was implemented), that the 'great men' were 'posting to London for places and honours, every man full of his own merit, and afraid of every one near him'. Defoe's allegations are confirmed by the Earl of Godolphin, who at the end of April reported from London that the business of settling the financial affairs of Scotland, 'as well as the adjusting of the pretensions of all the Scots men new here', was proving difficult.[8] The notion that corruption had played a crucial, if sordid, role in the surrender of Scotland's parliamentary independence periodically recurred through the eighteenth and early nineteenth centuries. Its presence in the poetry of Robert Burns and Robert Fergusson has already been noted, but it also appears in Sir Walter Scott's *Tales of A Grandfather*, a lengthy section of which (despite Scott's belief in the necessity and, latterly with less enthusiasm, the virtue of the Union) denigrates Scotland's 'false and corrupted statesmen'. Although accusations of betrayal – and indeed anti-Union sentiments – were less commonly heard in Victorian Scotland, they did not disappear entirely.[9]

Pro-Union historians have been the most vocal critics of what they have seen as a slur on the motives of those who voted for the various stages by which the union legislation passed through the Scottish Parliament between 1705 and 1707. Thus James MacKinnon, in his scholarly and lucid *Union of England and Scotland: A Study of International*

History (1896), still one of the best books on the subject, was at
considerable pains to contradict the accusation made by George
Lockhart of Carnwath, not long after 1707, that a sum of over
£20,000 had been obtained from Queen Anne and the English
Treasury and secretly distributed in Scotland by the Earl of Glasgow,
the Scottish Treasurer-Depute. This, it was alleged, was to secure
support for the Union proposal, or in Lockhart's words, for the
purpose of 'promoting His [Glasgow's] Countries Ruine and
Misery'.[10] As the payments were secret, and not officially accounted
for, some individuals, according to Lockhart, were paid twice.

Although Lockhart had (to his own great surprise) been appointed
as one of the Commissioners for a treaty of union in March 1706,
he was, as has been noted, an opponent of incorporating union.
Accordingly, MacKinnon was able to dismiss Lockhart as 'partisan',
and declared that he was 'not prepared to find a large body of
Scottish statesmen bartering the independence of their country at the
price of a few hundred pounds each'.[11] He then went on to refute
Lockhart's charges one by one, by pointing out, for instance, that the
sums were payments of arrears due to servants of the Crown, and
that the £12,325 which was paid to the Duke of Queensberry, the
Queen's Commissioner in the 1706 session of the Scottish Parliament,
was not an unreasonable sum for his official expenses. The remaining
£8,000, divided according to Lockhart between another 30 individuals, some of whom received £50 or less, was of little significance to
MacKinnon. (A full list of the payments and their recipients can be
seen in P. W. J. Riley's *The Union of England and Scotland*.) Lockhart's
assertion, that these sums did matter, merited 'ridicule rather than
indignation'. MacKinnon's protestations continued to find support
amongst respectable historians: thus, while Hume Brown was unable
to discount the possibility that some members had been bribed, to
suggest that bribery 'carried the Union' was 'absurd'.[12]

A more effective defence would have been that the Scots were
perhaps only playing with particular vigour the contemporary political game, introduced to win support for the King at Westminster
after the Restoration, and used with effect by the strengthening
Court party. In Scotland patronage had frequently been used to help
smooth the course of political events in the seventeenth century.[13] By

the early 1700s, management and corruption were entrenched within the British political system, and benefits in the forms of bribes, sinecures and pensions had become integral parts of the political currency. They continued to be used until after the 1832 Reform Act. Thus the point was fairly made by Pryde and others, that the offer of rewards in return for political services was simply part of the routine political methods of the day. Moral outrage at the behaviour of certain Scottish politicians should therefore be muted, and their actions judged by the standards of the early eighteenth century, not those which (in theory at least) are applicable nowadays.

This is not to suggest that what to modern eyes appear as more dubious forms of political management should be ignored; far from it. It is essential to our understanding of how the union arrangements were steered through the Scottish Parliament. Indeed from the 1960s bribery began to re-emerge on the historiographical stage. The leading proponents of this rather more cynical (or perhaps realistic?) school of thought, a Scottish variant of Sir Lewis Namier's debunking approach to eighteenth-century politicians and political history, have been, first and foremost, Dr William Ferguson, of Edinburgh University; the late Dr P. W. J. Riley, at the University of Manchester; and the active Scottish Nationalist writer, P. H. Scott.

Ferguson's seminal book on the Union, *Scotland's Relations With England*, first appeared in 1977, although he had begun his aggressive assault on received opinions earlier, in an article published by *The Scottish Historical Review* in 1964. In his publications Ferguson countered all forms of historical determinism as they affected interpretations of the Union of 1707, and argued instead that those who took the 'long' view of the Union (i.e. believed that there was a certain inevitability about it) ignored three things. Two of these are of immediate relevance. The third was the ineffectiveness of the divided opposition forces, or what has recently been described as the 'political ineptitude' of the Scottish Parliament.[14] In this respect even 'the Patriot', Fletcher of Saltoun, must bear his fair share of the blame. Although elected a member of the Scottish Parliament in 1703, he was unable to settle in Scotland for long, preferring the greater opportunities there were abroad to buy and read books and examine fine buildings (those historians who are supremely confident about Scotland's material

achievements by the end of the seventeenth century might ask themselves where was Scotland's equivalent of the rows of opulent
merchant residences built alongside Amsterdam's Heerengracht canal
from the 1610s?). Livelier discussion and debate were to be found in
London coffee houses and those of the other European cities. Fletcher
was his own man, who found it difficult to maintain friends or
supporters. In parliamentary debates he was outstanding and greatly
admired, but also prone to lose his temper, and the respect of his
fellows.[15]

Ferguson placed most stress on improved political management
after 1704, although such a system, he readily admitted, had necessarily operated in Scotland at least since the Union of the Crowns in
1603. What was crucial about 1704, however, was the demonstration
of parliamentary independence on the part of the Scots, backed, it
appears, by a powerful surge of patriotic sentiment in the wider
community. Contrary to English wishes, the Scottish Parliament had
in 1703 passed the Act of Security, which not only gave to the Scots
the right to decide who should succeed the heirless Queen Anne (the
last of her children had died, aged eleven, in 1700), but also laid
down conditions – 'limitations' – under which they would accept a
monarch of England. The royal assent, however, had not been
forthcoming. In 1704, an uncompromising Scottish Parliament forced
the Queen and her Scottish Commissioner the Marquess of
Tweeddale to assent, reluctantly, to the Act of Security.

Thenceforth, the English determined to ensure that Anne's successor
was a Protestant and a Hanoverian, and further, that the Scottish
Parliament's powers should be curtailed – if not liquidated altogether –
by a parliamentary or incorporating union. Various means were
adopted in order to achieve this, amongst which were 'inducements' to
the noble members of Parliament.[16] By this Ferguson meant the use of
patronage and influence, which, in a well-known example, saw the
Duke of Argyll, the Queen's former Commissioner, whose support was
required in Edinburgh, agreeing to return to Scotland from the front at
Flanders (where he was serving with the Duke of Marlborough's army)
after being told 'what to expect for going'. He obtained an English
peerage and was promoted to the rank of Major-General. Secondly,
there was the role of more blatant forms of bribery, referred to above,

the extent of which led Ferguson to describe the Union as the greatest 'political job' of the eighteenth century.

Looking closely at the evidence, historians discovered a number of warts on the previously unblemished portraits of prominent Scottish politicians, even though many of these could have been highlighted earlier. Much of the evidence was there (but largely ignored), in the published collections of contemporary correspondence, for example. Although some new sources have come to light, changes in the attitudes and interests of historians have been equally important. Thus, far from being an 'architect' of incorporating union, the Duke of Queensberry was in the 1960s being depicted as an opportunist, who, forced from office in May 1704, joined the opposition forces: during the parliamentary session of 1704 his supporters 'engaged in a deliberate campaign to sabotage the New Party [the administration party now led by John Hay, 2nd Marquess of Tweeddale, see below] and the English court.[17] The reputations of others too – the Earls of Glasgow and Cromartie are good examples – are badly tarnished, as historians have exposed their opportunism and the facility they demonstrated in changing their colours according to which way they thought the wind of personal political advantage was blowing.

It is argued too that sums which in £ sterling may appear inconsequential, meant a lot more to avaricious contemporaries who were both desperately short of specie, and conducted their financial affairs in pounds Scots. Even the most affluent landowner required quantities of coin in order to participate in Scottish life and society, to pay for small expenses such as beard trimming, horse hire and feed, ale and subsistence when travelling, and tips. £50 – or even the paltry £11 2s paid to Lord Banff – looks rather more when multiplied by 12, which was the rate at which English currency was converted into Scots.

P. H. Scott has taken the investigations of Ferguson and Riley further, and discovered other instances where financial inducements appear to have aided the pro-Union cause. William Seton of Pitmedden, for example, evidently had good reason for shifting his ground. In July 1704 he had been a vocal supporter of federal union and sided with the opposition, but from 1705 he wrote and spoke in the most persuasive terms in support of an incorporating union. A request made on his behalf in November 1704 to the Earl of Seafield,

Lord High Chancellor in the Scottish Parliament, for a pension of £100 a year had been successful.[18] More significant, however, is the evidence Scott adduces in favour of the view that the Duke of Hamilton was bribed or otherwise persuaded at key moments to act in ways which appeared to be at odds with his conscience and his supporters – and against the wishes of his spirited, politically con-scious and highly patriotic mother. The precise nature of the part played by Duchess Anne in Scottish politics, conducted very much in the background, remains unclear and its importance unmeasured, although a recent attempt has been made to assess the political role of two of her three daughters, both of whom were enraged by England's attitude to and actions concerning Darien.[19] The nature and impact of the contribution of females of all ranks in the making of the Act of Union is one which would be well worth examining.

The behaviour of James, 4th Duke of Hamilton, in the immediate pre-Union years has long puzzled historians. Hamilton was the nominal leader of the opposition Country Party, with a slim claim to the throne himself (by descent from the royal line). He was immensely popular with the crowds outside Parliament, who were strongly opposed to closer (incorporating) union with Scotland's old enemy England. So, too, it would appear, was Hamilton, who had played a prominent part in the independently inclined Parliament of 1704. In February 1705 he assured his mother, Duchess Anne, that 'noe body needs take any paines with me', about what form a treaty with England should take: he had long been convinced that 'what has been the source of our ruine since our king's becam thers' was that 'wee had not stipulations made with them'. That which was 'now called a treaty of union is a treaty of subjugation and not of union'.[20] His mother was in agreement and, conscious of and not a little concerned by the popular 'ferment' against the settlement which she observed in Hamilton and believed to be nationwide, chastised her son and his allies in November 1706 for not sending a representative to the Queen and acquainting her 'how ye nation is disposed agn't this union'.[21]

Yet at key moments, when Hamilton's intervention on the opposi-tion side could have been decisive, he failed his intensely loyal supporters and came to the aid of the Court. For this reason, somewhat paradoxically, he has been credited with helping the unionists. Arguably the most critical occasion when he let his own side down was on 1 September 1705, when Parliament was preparing to vote on whether the nominations for the Scottish Commissioners who were to negotiate the conditions of the proposed treaty of union should be decided by Parliament or the Queen. At the last minute, inexplicably, Hamilton proposed that they should be the Queen's nominees, thereby ensuring that they would also be pro-union, much to the chagrin of opposition MPs. George Lockhart remarked that from this day 'may we date the Commencement of *Scotland's* Ruine'.[22]

Later, in November, it was evidently Hamilton who gave orders that a planned rising of Covenanters in the south-west, along with some parties of Jacobites, including the Highlanders of the Duke of Atholl (another magnate and outspoken opponent of incorporating union), should be called off. The most notorious instance, however, was early in January 1707, when Hamilton played a leading part in the campaign for a 'Protestation' to be delivered to the Queen, expressing opposition to the proposed incorporating union and intimating the refusal of its adherents to accept the proposed British Parliament. Having marshalled considerable support, however, at the last minute, Hamilton refused to attend the House, 'pretending to be seized of the Toothache'.

Hamilton was both heavily in debt and had acquired, through marriage, estates in Lancashire in England. He had much to gain if he could persuade English ministers that his support was worth purchasing, something which he appears to have done in a highly secretive manner, without the knowledge even of the Scottish officers of state – with the exception of James Johnstone, Lord Clerk Register, who was 'certain' in January 1705 that Hamilton was 'tampering' with Robert Harley, the English minister, to have his debts paid.[23] Others observed from a distance, and came to their own conclusions: 'I knew that this Duke was so unlucky in his privat circumstances that he wou'd have complied with any thing on a suitable encouragement' was Sir John Clerk's terse but revealing comment.

It is clear too that Hamilton had not a little to lose either, and his English properties would have been seriously endangered had the Aliens Act of 1705 (see Chapter 3) come into force. In short, although the evidence is not altogether conclusive, there is sufficient of it to take extremely seriously the accusation that Hamilton perceived that his best interests lay in supporting Queen Anne and her ministers' wishes for Scotland, and followed them, whatever the eventual cost to his political and personal credibility. Or, as it has been put by John S. Gibson, 'An incorporating Union would bring no crown to the house of Hamilton, but in time there would be pickings'.[24]

Political management, then, in its various forms, played a part in securing a majority in the Scottish Parliament for incorporating union. It is not easy, however, to determine how much emphasis should be placed on it. Not all modern historians have been prepared to accord a decisive role to bribery.

Seton of Pitmedden, for instance, had apparently first gone into print on behalf of an incorporating union in 1700, on the grounds that it would benefit Scotland's underdeveloped economy.[25] Professor Rosalind Mitchison remains convinced by the argument that the sums paid out of the infamous £20,000 were relatively small, and represented salary arrears, as had long been claimed by pro-unionists.[26] Professor T. C. Smout, in one of the most frequently quoted essays on the causes of the Union, declared that even if bribery on a wide scale could be proved, it was difficult to show that this had determined how someone had actually voted. Furthermore, he went on, it is 'almost impossible to establish for any individual that he changed his mind as a result of receiving a bribe'.[27]

Subsequent research has eroded the force of the last of these claims. There were others – apart from Hamilton – who appear to have supported the Court against their usual political inclinations. One of the most convincing examples is Alexander Murray, 4th Baron Elibank.[28] Other former opponents were Sir Kenneth Mackenzie of Cromartie, and the 11th Earl of Glencairn, who received 100 pounds Scots and was also threatened with the loss of his pension from the civil list.[29] Members of the Squadrone Volante (who also received some of the biggest payments from the £20,000) benefited too from military patronage.

The significance of the Squadrone Volante requires to be emphasised. Although without the formal structure, organisation or discipline of British political parties as they emerged in the nineteenth century, there were, roughly speaking, three party groupings in the pre-1707 Parliament. Just the largest, the Court Party, included the officers of state and other London appointees and acted and governed on behalf of the monarch. The opposition comprised the Country Party, and the smaller Cavalier Party, whose members were effectively Jacobites, wanted to restore the Stuart line. A 'New Party', which became known as the Squadrone Volante, an offshoot of the Country Party, was formed in 1704, led by the Marquess of Tweeddale. Although anxious to promote an image of political reasonableness and concern for Scotland's future, this was probably misleading.[30] The support of the two dozen or so members of the Squadrone Volante was vital to the Court. They held the balance, and without their votes, as has long been recognised, the union proposals would have been blocked in the Scottish Parliament. Their support for incorporating union represented a major shift of position, as when in office in 1704 and 1705 the New Party's objective had been to carry the Hanoverian succession, but not a treaty of union. It also bore a high price, in the form of 'bargains'.

It should be noted, however, that Smout's doubts, which were of the views expressed by Ferguson in his 1964 *Scottish Historical Review* article, were published prior to the publication of substantial books by both Ferguson and Riley. They also predated Scott. Even so, while subsequent research has taken some of the sting out of Smout's criticisms, other questions he raised are still worth asking: for example, why, if the Union was a 'political job', did Westminster feel it necessary to make so many concessions to the Scots – in allowing the Presbyterian Church to retain its independence, for example, or the preservation of the Scottish legal system? Why did the English negotiators concede a 'number of significant economic details' as the Articles went through the Parliament of Scotland during November and December 1706 (see below); and, finally, why was Daniel Defoe engaged to come to Scotland to embark on a vigorous propaganda campaign? It is worth noting, too, that despite the fact that Seton of Pitmedden had allegedly been 'bought', the recently published letters of George Lockhart of Carnwath reveal that he did not surrender his integrity, but was prepared to join forces with Lockhart in 1706 in the meetings of the Commissioners for union to argue for additional relief from English taxes.[31]

Indeed, an innovative computer analysis of voting patterns of the Scottish 'estates' has revealed that there was a 'level of principled commitment to Union hitherto underplayed . . . by historians'. The main ground for this claim is the voting record of thirteen members of the Scottish Parliament who 'can be identified as supporting the Union consistently without benefit of office, financial inducement, committee service, or ties of kinship', although eleven of them were subsequently rewarded in one way or another.[32] Although the number of principled members was thus small, that they existed should be acknowledged. What is also underlined is the failure of the opposition forces (the use of the concept of an opposition *party* is largely misleading) to marshal their supporters on key issues, with nineteen Jacobites, for instance, failing to vote against the ratification of the Union. Yet there were men of principle on the opposition side, although Andrew Fletcher of Saltoun's Constitutional Reformers, who voted fairly consistently against the Court, comprised only fifteen men. In addition, however, there were a further twelve nobles, led by the Earl of Errol and hitherto undifferentiated from the inconsistent (or 'indulgent') Countrymen, who had an even more solid record of opposition. It is notable, for example, that the Duke of Atholl was a consistent opponent of union in spite of the fact that he would benefit from the opening up of trade: 'leaving the Politicks . . . I doe nothing doubt', he was advised by Sir John Cochrane, 'but your Grace will finde the advantage of a Communication of trade in the seal [sic] of your Linning Cloth and Cattel'.[33] Atholl was also due to receive £1,500 from the Equivalent, for government service in 1703–4. In short, the more inflated claims which have been made about the extent and depth of Scottish venality – based in part on English caricature (and the demand of Scots post-1707 for scapegoats) – need to be scaled down.

Moreover, although it is highly unlikely that many of the leading Court figures who on behalf of Queen Anne and latterly the English Whig majority steered the union legislation through the Scottish Parliament did so on the basis of what they foresaw of Scotland's long-term prospects, there is even amongst nationalist historians a recognition that those involved 'were not entirely moved by self-interest, but had thought deeply and were concerned about the fate of Scotland'.[34] Indeed there were those – such as the 1st Earl of Stair and his brother Sir David Dalrymple – who had been committed (incorporating) unionists long before the autumn of 1705. Stair himself spoke effectively in favour, without reward.[35] This, however, was unusual. Nevertheless, although Lockhart of Carnwath's penetrating descriptions of the motives and characteristics of men such as the Earl of Cromartie ('there never was a more fickle, unsteady man in the world') or the Duke of Argyll ('capable of the worst things to promote his interest') provide powerful antidotes to the temptation to use the term 'statesmen' without substantial qualification, there is much substance in the older argument that there was a growing recognition that a treaty of some sort with England was necessary if relations with England were not to worsen. This fear was ably-expressed by Cromartie who, despite his alleged weaknesses, firmly rejected the federal option on the grounds that 'Unless we be a part each of other, the union will be as a blood puddin to bind a cat, i.e., till one or the other be hungry, and then the puddin flies'.[36] Seton of Pitmedden, one of the Scottish Commissioners selected by the monarch to negotiate the Treaty of Union, saw advantages for Britain, but also for Scotland, in the form of protection from her enemies. Whether or not he believed it in 1705 and 1706, one of Sir John Clerk's justifications for the Union, grounded in his period as a student at Leiden and his study of Grotius, was that Britain, as an island, had been formed by Nature (God) to be an independent entity under a single government.[37] 'A plurality of small states', he wrote, was relatively weak, unlike Queen Anne's creation, the bigger and therefore stronger *imperium Britannicum*. Others came round more slowly, but were eventually convinced that incorporation was the only workable solution – which might have real benefits, such as the Earl of Roxburghe's belief that union would prevent a Jacobite restoration as English troops would be able to move freely in Scotland.

Indeed there was a fear in some quarters that if agreement was not reached, England would resort to a military solution. As will be seen in the following chapter, England's political ambitions demanded that the Scots agree to the Hanoverian succession and an incorporating union. Whether the English would actually have been 'foolish' enough to have embarked on such a course of action is less clear.[38] For most of the period 1689 to 1714 British troops were committed to a level of direct involvement on the Continent that had only been seen previously in the Middle Ages and, after occupying Madrid in June 1706, began to struggle in their Spanish campaign. But there is no doubt that English troops were being marshalled near to the Border in November 1706, as well as in Ireland, partly as a result of concerns in London, not so much about the Scottish Parliament, where by this time there was a majority in favour of the Union, but the reports that were being received about a threatened popular revolt, which might have enabled the Jacobite genie to emerge from what remained an unstable lamp.[39] But there were many Scots too – Roxburghe has just been mentioned – who shared this anxiety.

It is difficult to decide what emphasis should be placed on what have been described as the 'striking and sophisticated' arguments of pamphleteers such as Seton of Pitmedden and George MacKenzie, Viscount Tarbat (from 1703, 1st Earl of Cromartie), which it has been claimed (by John Robertson, for example, an eminent historian of political thought) have been overlooked by those historians who have been 'obsessed' by bribery. Clearly there were powerfully articulated arguments in favour of union (see Appendix I) – and against. That there was an energetic 'pamphlet war' suggests that there was an interested audience in Scotland, which men like Defoe and the learned Fletcher believed was worth addressing. There is considerable evidence, including the recently discovered petition to Parliament from the boys of Canongate School in Edinburgh, that the Union was a much-discussed issue.[40] Parliamentarians too evidently believed in the value of the written word, rewarding two writers, James Anderson (a staunch advocate of Scottish independence) and James Hodges, whose views they favoured, with 4,800 pounds Scots each in August 1705, while 'scurrilous' books which were 'full of falsehoods . . . reflecting on the honour and independency' of Scotland were ordered to be burned. One of the most significant was that written by the English whig historian William Attwood – who argued, dangerously, as far as the Scots were concerned, that as the Scottish Crown had always been dependent on England, the Scots had no right to challenge the Act of Settlement.[41] Underlining the potential danger contemporaries recognised in the written word, the pro-union

Presbytery of Arbroath ordered their brethren to suppress what 'erroneous books they can hear of'.[42]

It is much harder still to assess the impact which the work of the pamphleteers had inside Parliament. Clearly the anti-unionists and federalists made little headway, even though most of the petitions which were dispatched to Edinburgh argued rather than simply asserted their sponsors' positions through weight of the number of signatures. But what about writers such as Defoe and Pitmedden? The evidence currently available is that the written word played only a minor role in determining the voting behaviour of the great majority of Scottish parliamentarians during the final months of 1706. Examination of what they actually did rather than what was written, read and discussed shows that despite shifting associations and cross-voting, 'political affiliations based on adherence to party were measurably the most cohesive, comprehensive and cogent influences on voting'.[43] This does not exclude the possibility that pro-Union voters were also influenced by those writers whose pragmatism drove them to conclude that Union was the only option left after the failure of Darien. Others, persuaded that it was the fabric of Scottish society, and the poverty of its agriculture, rather than England or regal union that lay at the root of Scotland's ills, advocated the same solution as a means of achieving national renewal.[44] Nevertheless, the modern consensus suggests that however powerful the pro-unionist case, bribery was still required to shore up the support of the waverers in the Court camp; indeed it is not considered unreasonable to suspect that the role of financial inducements was rather more substantial.[45]

Such inducements were not always negotiated secretly. As will be seen later, particular private interests were enshrined within the Articles of Union themselves. Self-interest played its part in other ways too, with the union Commissioners apparently being persuaded to accept that only 16 Scottish peers would sit in the House of Lords, as long as the rest enjoyed the immunities and privileges enjoyed by their English counterparts. Amongst these – which the Scots did not have – were immunity from arrest and civil actions involving debt. It has been suggested that the 'poverty which made them vulnerable to bribery also made them susceptible to the offer of freedom from the debtors' prison', which more than compensated them for their loss of political representation.[46]

At a more general level, however, one of the most persuasive Articles was the XVth, which dealt with the Equivalent. The sum of money this represented, just over £398,000, was agreed to by the English in June 1706, and was to compensate the Scots for under taking to repay part of England's national debt. Amongst the purposes to which it was to be put was the repayment of the capital stock of the failed Company of Scotland Trading to Africa and the Indies (founded in 1695), plus interest at five per cent per annum. The Company's high hopes had been dashed when English investors withdrew because of fears that the Scottish venture would pose a threat to the East India Company. Nevertheless, Scottish mercantilist hopes of developing the country's overseas trade, backed by patriotic fervour, gave rise to the so-called Darien Scheme, whereby a trading colony was to be established on the Isthmus of Panama at Darien. For several reasons, it turned out to be a 'tragic farce', with much loss of life, capital and capital equipment, such as ships.[47]

The damage to the Scottish economy was substantial. The £153,000 (1.8 million pounds Scots) of paid-up capital which disappeared represented perhaps as much as one-quarter of the country's liquid capital. The investors who had lost most, by contributing almost half of the Darien funds, were the landed classes (with members of the Squadrone Volante being particularly deeply involved). They were strongly represented in Parliament, and the suggestion that their losses would be made good by union (the first hint to this effect was heard in 1702), with not only their capital being repaid, but with an additional five per cent interest, thus represented a considerable inducement to them to support the measure. Lockhart of Carnwath was less circumspect and called the Equivalent 'a clear bribe' which was designed to buy off the Scottish members of Parliament.[48] With compensation also to be paid under the terms of the Equivalent to individuals who would lose when the Scottish currency was called in and replaced by the English, the description of the Equivalent as 'the price of Scotland' carries no little conviction today. It is to be regretted that detailed accounts which set actual losses against eventual reimbursements appear not to have survived, except that what mattered to those concerned was the promise that they would be compensated, not what they eventually received. Thus members of the Squadrone had been promised that they would be given the oversight of the payments from the Equivalent made to Darien shareholders. Later on, however, the Court reneged, preferring instead to appoint a commission which would be responsible to the British Parliament.

Nevertheless, a modest but welcome attempt to assess the extent to which those who voted for or against the Union has recently been made, using only voting records on the 1st Article (which created a single kingdom of Great Britain), and a variety of financial records of varying quality.[49] The results are not as conclusive as might be wished, and are capable of bearing unexpected or even unwelcome conclusions, depending on the reader's point of view.

Thus the evidence relating to Darien stockholders who voted on the 1st Article suggests that, amongst the nobility, a disproportionately high share of the compensation for Darien (69 per cent), to which the nobility were entitled, went to those who had voted 'yes'. Analysis of the burgh commissioners' votes on the other hand shows that the noes accounted for a significantly higher proportion of the Darien compensation due to the burghs. However, this may not be indicative of a greater degree of altruism on the part of the burghs. Rather, it suggests that the burgh representatives were aware of Article XXII which, by cutting the number of these in the House of Commons to 45, would have removed from the Scottish burghs – Edinburgh excepted – their independent representation at Westminster. In other words, there were issues which determined voting patterns other than the size of the financial reward, a point underlined by the fact that a number of burgh commissioners voted against the instructions of their burgh councils, and joined with their friends or connections amongst the peerage in voting for the 1st Article. The burgh of Brechin provides an example of another aspect of the same problem. Brechin had a relatively large stake in Darien, and instructed their commissioner, Francis Mollison, to vote for. He voted against. Unproven, but suggestive, is another point made by the author of these findings, John Shaw. It is that while amongst the nobility there was clearly some support for the Union based on the size of Darien stockholdings and the promise of a healthy return, if, as has rightly been argued, the Darien venture was partly supported for patriotic reasons, it is tempting to suggest that at least some of those who had invested in Darien, and who also voted yes in 1706, were the genuine Scottish patriots, who had not been afraid to open their purses in support of their dreams.[50]

There can be no doubt, however, that the Court used all the means of patronage it had at its disposal in order to carry the Union. The union Commissioners were rewarded with hefty fees (£30,300 sterling in total). Even Lockhart of Carnwath received £600. High Commissioners in the Scottish Parliament also did well, in particular Queensberry, who was also made Duke of Dover in May 1708. Earlier, other significant elevations to the peerage were made: Argyll (Earl of Greeenwich), and his brother Archibald Campbell (Earl of Ilay), Lord Henry Scott, son of the Duchess of Buccleuch and the Duke of Monmouth (Earl of Deloraine), while dukedoms were awarded to Montrose and Roxburghe, of the Squadrone Volante. Sometimes these individuals, and others, received additional gifts too, of feu duties for example, or, in the case of the Earl of Morton, renewal of his royal charter of the earldom of Orkney. But even though the value of such awards to their recipients was substantial, doubts remain about how the evidence should be interpreted. Many pensions and other sums due from the civil list were paid to persons too low down the social scale to affect the outcome of the Union votes; it was prudent for the Scots commissioners to negotiate a settlement of Scotland's public debts during 1706; not all payments were made to 'yes' voters – others who benefited from the payment of arrears from the Equivalent included the Earl of Buchan and John Forbes of Culloden (both 'no' voters).[51]

Party Advantage

P. W. J. Riley, whose work has already been noted in passing, was equally unimpressed by arguments which presented the Union as the outcome of wise and forward-looking political endeavour. He was dismissive, too, of explanations which assume that the process was inevitable. He was also one of those historians who took issue with the argument that 1707 was simply an 'incident' in a long-run process of political, economic and cultural assimilation, a 'tradition of states-manship', according to Dicey and Rait, 'which stretches over a period of at least four hundred years ... from the accession of Edward I (1272) till about the middle of the reign of Anne (1707)'. Rather, Riley claimed, the Union, on both sides of the border, 'was made by men of limited vision for very short-term and comparatively petty, if not squalid, aims'.[52] It was also part of his purpose to consider the Union as a formative event in British political history, an approach which has recently been re-emphasised by John Morrill.

In a richly detailed book, Riley argued that King William's English Whig ministers, who before around 1700 had shown little interest in Scottish politics, and saw no point in union, began to undergo a dramatic change of mind. A union would resolve the succession problem, as in 1689 the Scottish parliament had asserted the right to decide who their monarch was independently. Union might also bring sympathetic Scotsmen into a House of Commons in which the Whigs were outnumbered by their Tory rivals. (The Triennial Act of 1694 had had a 'dynamic' effect on English politics and government, not the least significant aspect of which was to increase the number of elections and thereby intensify party rivalry.) Although a change in circumstances – the accession to the throne of Queen Anne and a Tory administration (which saw no benefit in a closer connection with Presbyterian Scotland) – caused the Whigs to drop their interest, this had revived again by 1706. The new English Parliament which first met in October 1705 had a Whig majority. Support for the war and a determination to deal with 'Scottish intransigence and sheer irresponsibility' brought the prospect of incorporating union to the fore.[53]

Pressure from England for incorporating union was in large part driven by the strategic need to remove the root cause of Anglo-Scottish quarrels – the separate Scottish legislature. However, the Treaty itself was negotiated on the English side by the Whig 'junto', but not 'for the sake of posterity: they were concerned with the political balance at Westminster in the immediate future'.[54] Yet at the same time, and because of his fears of growing 'junto' strength, it appears that Harley, commonly credited with being the most active pro-union English minister, appears to have become much less enthusiastic. Busily 'scavenging what they could on the fringes of this rivalry were the main Scottish interests'. Amongst these was the concern of sections of the Scottish nobility that Queen Anne's successor should not be James VIII and III, the exiled Stuart monarch, which was a possible consequence of the Act of Security. In turn this would have put at risk the ascendancy of the Presbyterian church and 'the political power of those nobles who had supported the post-revolutionary administration'.[55] Yet all the indications are that even in the summer of 1705, the English Court would have settled for a resolution of the Succession question without a parliamentary union.[56] Viewed in this light, until the end of 1705 that a parliamentary union would be proposed was by no means cut and dried, and even then, as will be argued below, further work was necessary on the part of the Court in Scotland to ensure the desired outcome. Nevertheless, it can reasonably be objected that Riley's approach was too cynical and, by looking too narrowly at the minutiae of political affairs, he failed to discern the greater political benefits to both countries which were observed by at least some contemporaries.

NOTES TO CHAPTER 2

1. P. Hume Brown, *History of Scotland to the Present Time* (Cambridge, 1911), III, 101.
2. G. S. Pryde, *Scotland from 1603 to the Present Day* (London, 1962), 55.
3. W. L. Mathieson, *Scotland and the Union: A History of Scotland from 1695 to 1747* (Glasgow, 1905), 148.
4. Hume Brown, *History of Scotland*, 117–18.
5. M. Ash, *The Strange Death of Scottish History* (Edinburgh, 1980), 146–8.
6. See L. Colley, *Britons. Forging the Nation, 1707–1837* (New Haven and London, 1992).
7. Blair Castle, Atholl MSS, (6) 129, Ann Hay to the Duke of Atholl, 5 December 1706.
8. H. L. Snyder (ed.), *The Marlborough-Godolphin Correspondence* (3 vols, Oxford, 1975), 2, 754–5.

9. Ash, *Strange Death of Scottish History*, 137–8; the best recent writing on the struggles Scott had to grapple with over the issues of Union and national betrayal is Iwazumi, 'The Union of 1707', 13–36.

10. G. Lockhart, *Memoirs Concerning the Affairs of Scotland From Queen Anne's Accession to the Throne To The Commencement of the Union of the Two Kingdoms of England and Scotland* (London, 1714), 413.

11. MacKinnon, *The Union of England and Scotland: A Study in International History* (London, 1896) 343.

12. Hume Brown, *History of Scotland*, 101.

13. K. Brown, *Kingdom or Province? Scotland and the Regal Union, 1603–1715* (London, 1992), 41.

14. Macinnes, 'Politically Reactionary Brits?: The promotion of Anglo-Scottish Union, 1603–1715', in S. J. Connolly (ed.), *Kingdoms United? Great Britain and Ireland since 1500: Integration and Diversity* (Dublin, 1999) (London, 1992), 54.

15. See Robertson, *Andrew Fletcher: Political Works* (Cambridge, 1997), xii–xv.

16. W. Ferguson, 'The Making of the Treaty of Union', *Scottish Historical Review*, XLIII (1964), 97–108.

17. Riley, *The Union of England and Scotland: A Study in Anglo-Scottish Politics of the Eighteenth Century* (Manchester, 1978), 107.

18. P. H. Scott, *Andrew Fletcher and the Treaty of Union* (Edinburgh, 1992), 119.

19. See K. von den Steinen, 'In Search of the Antecedents of Women's Political Activism in Early Eighteenth-Century Scotland: the Daughters of Anne, Duchesss of Hamilton', in E. Ewen and M. M. Meikle (eds.), *Women in Scotland, c.1100–c.1750* (East Linton, 1999), 112–22.

20. National Archives of Scotland, Hamilton MSS, GD406/1/10344, Duke of Hamilton to the Duchess, 11 February 1705.

21. Ibid, GD406/1/9733, Duchess of Hamilton to Duke, 16 November 1706.

22. Lockhart, *Memoirs*, 172.

23. Scott, *Andrew Fletcher*, 140–4.

24. J. S. Gibson, *Playing the Scottish Card: The Franco-Jacobite Invasion of 1708* (Edinburgh, 1988), 62–7.

25. J. Robertson, 'Andrew Fletcher's Vision of Union', in R. A. Mason (ed.), *Scotland and England, 1286–1815* (Edinburgh, 1987), 208.

26. R. Mitchison, *Lordship to Patronage: Scotland 1603–1745* (London, 1983), 134.

27. T. C. Smout, 'The Road to Union', in G. Holmes (ed.), *Britain after the Glorious Revolution* (London, 1969), 190.

28. Riley, *Union of England and Scotland*, 258.

29. A. I. Macinnes, 'Studying the Scottish Estates and the Treaty of Union', *History Microcomputer Review*, 6 (Fall, 1990), 14.

30. Riley, *Union of England and Scotland*, 262.

31. D. Szechi (ed.), *Letters of George Lockhart of Carnwath, 1698–1732* (Edinburgh,1989), 31–3.

32. Macinnes, 'Studying the Scottish Estates', 19.

33. Blair Castle, Atholl MSS, (7) 18, Sir John Cochrane to the Duke of Atholl, 3 April 1707.

34. Scott, *Andrew Fletcher*, 164.

35. W. L. Mathieson, *Scotland and the Union*, 151–4; additional support for this assessment of Stair is provided in Clerk, *History of the Union* (n. 37 below).

36. Quoted in Riley, *Union of England and Scotland*, 183.

37. Sir John Clerk, *History of the Union of Scotland and England* (Edinburgh, 1993), 9, 33–35.

38. B. Lenman, *An Economic History of Modern Scotland, 1660–1976* (London, 1977), 57.

39. H. L. Snyder (ed.), *The Marlborough-Godolphin Correspondence* (3 vols., Oxford, 1975), II, 727; see too J. R. Young, 'The Parliamentary Incorporating Union of 1707: Political Management, Anti-Unionism and Foreign Policy', in T. M. Devine and J. R. Young (eds.), *Eighteenth-Century Scotland: New Perspectives* (East Linton, 1999), 40–46.

40. NAS, Hamilton MSS, GD 406/M9/247/18, Petition against the Union, 1706.

41. C. Kidd, *Subverting Scotland's Past: Scottish Whig Historians and the Creation of an Anglo-British Identity* (Cambridge, 1993), 45.

42. G. Hay, *History of Arbroath* (Arbroath, 1876), 165.

43. Macinnes, 'Studying the Scottish Estates', 15.

44. C. Kidd, 'North Britishness and the nature of eighteenth-century British patriotisms', *Historical Journal*, 39 (1996), 367.

45. Brown, *Kingdom or Province?*, 191; M. Lynch, *Scotland: A New History* (London, 1991), 312.

46. Scott, *Andrew Fletcher*, 157.

47. T. C. Smout, *Scottish Trade on the Eve of Union, 1660–1707* (Edinburgh, 1963), 252.

48. D. Szechi (ed.), *Letters of George Lockhart of Carnwath*, 33.

49. What follows is drawn from J. S. Shaw, *The Political History of Eighteenth-Century Scotland* (Basingstoke, 1999), 1–17.

50. Ibid., 1–11.

51. Ibid., 12–17.

52. Riley, *Union of England and Scotland*, xvi, 2–3.

53. G. Holmes, *The Making of a Great Power: Late Stuart and Early Georgian Britain, 1660–1722* (London, 1993), 312.

54. Riley, *Union of England and Scotland*, 183.

55. I. B. Cowan, 'The Inevitability of Union – A Historical Fallacy?', *Scotia*, V (1991), 6.

56. NAS, GD1/1158/3, Lord Godolphin to the Duke of Argyll, 17 July 1705.

3

A Survey of Causes: Economic Arguments, England and Extra-Parliamentary Pressure

One of the most enduring explanations for the Union of 1707 is that Scotland exchanged (or bargained away) parliamentary sovereignty for free trade.[1] It is an idea that has a long pedigree. In a frequently quoted commentary, the Earl of Roxburghe, one of the leaders of the Squadrone Volante, placed trade at the forefront of his analysis of the reasons why his colleagues would vote in favour of incorporating union:

> The motives will be, Trade with most, Hanover with some, ease and security with others, together with a generall aversion at civill discords, intollerable poverty, and the constant oppression of a bad ministry, from generation to generation, without the least regard to the good of the country . . . [2]

Although Roxburghe's opinions were liable to alter, what is undeniable is that trade and Scotland's economic prospects figured prominently in debates, both inside Parliament and outside, whenever union with England – incorporating or otherwise – was discussed. Strictly speaking, however, it was not just *free* trade that the Scots wanted, it was *protected* trade. My critics are right to point out that there were fears in Scotland about the strength of English competition, but wrong to suppose that these were so strong that they outweighed the presumed advantages of the English connection. As will be shown below, vigorous efforts were made to protect some of the more vulnerable parts of the Scottish economy from English competition. Nevertheless, a constant irritant for historians who have attempted to incorporate economic concerns in their explanations for the Union of 1707, is the allegation that these are the inventions of later (Victorian and unionist) historians rather than matters in which contemporaries showed any interest. These issues will be dealt with in this chapter.

Economic Motives

Writing about the proposed union *in 1703*, Andrew Fletcher of Saltoun remarked that the prospect offered of expanded trade was 'the bait that covers the hook', and it has subsequently been argued that 'a whole school' of pamphleteers, including not only Daniel Defoe but also John Clerk of Penicuik, the Earl of Haddington, Thomas Coutts, and others, including Seton of Pitmedden, put their pens to work for this cause.[3] The importance of economic union to Scotland, through access to markets in England and English colonies, has been stressed by a long line of historians, from the nineteenth century right up to the present day. For MacKinnon this was the 'secret of union', while some ten years later W. L. Mathieson confidently asserted that, 'the arguments . . . which had most weight with the nation at large were the concession of that free commerce with England and her colonies which had been coveted and demanded in vain for nearly fifty years'.[4] More recently it has been claimed that 'the only truly persuasive arguments for union were economic'.[5]

By far the most convincing modern argument in favour of an economic motivation for the Union (or at least that economic factors were 'persuasively strong') has been developed by T. C. Smout, until recently the Professor of Scottish History at the University of St Andrews, and now Historiographer Royal. Almost forty years ago, Smout demonstrated not only that the Scottish economy had been strengthening (up to *c.*1680), but also that the export sector was becoming increasingly dependent on the English market. Something like half of Scotland's exports, he estimated, primarily linen and black cattle, were being sent to England by the end of the seventeenth century. Scotland's dependence, he argued, was greater because from the end of the 1670s a series of external blows wreaked havoc on the Scottish economy and exposed its underlying weaknesses: war with France had disrupted trade, while prohibition and tariffs, along with the rise of foreign competition, had had an adverse effect on important Scottish export commodities such as woollen cloth, fish, grain and coal. English commercial policy too was harmful to Scottish aspirations, with tariffs restricting several Scottish exports, while

Glasgow's embryonic trade with the Plantations was hit by the imposition of tighter regulations.[6]

Worse was to come. The first of a series of four major harvest failures occurred in 1695 and by the spring of 1700 the ill-fated Darien Scheme had failed. Squeezed out overseas, during the early years of the eighteenth century even the value of Scotland's exports to England began to fall off sharply. The effect of the Aliens Act, if implemented, would have been catastrophic, and Scottish trade, 'as it had developed in the seventeenth-century environment with its in-creasing dependence on England would have been decapitated', with little realistic hope of redeveloping trade along older, continental lines.[7]

In short, this argument runs, Scotland needed access to England and English markets overseas which were sheltered by the Navigation Acts. This, Smout was convinced, was recognised by the 'staunchest supporters of Union' in the Scottish Parliament, the nobility, the extent of whose direct involvement in the country's exports had not, he pointed out, been fully appreciated. Seeing that their interests lay in England therefore, with a few exceptions they voted for incorporat-ing union. One of the most articulate contemporary exponents of this line of reasoning was the aforementioned William Seton of Pitmedden, who argued that 'This nation, being poor, and without force to protect its commerce, cannot reap great advantage by it, till it partake of the trade and commerce of some powerful neighbour nation'.[8]

Smout was able to identify particular members of the nobility whose interests would be served by union. Amongst them was the Earl of Wemyss, whose overseas markets for coal and salt, 'were becoming more and more harassed', and who, Smout asserted, looked backwards to the Cromwellian Union when import duties into England had been lifted and Scottish sales soared, and deter-mined, when looking at their prospects for the future, to clutch at the straw of a new union. Similarly, the Earl of Cromartie and others with fertile grain-growing estates in the north-east needed the new market which England offered them.[9]

This was and still is a powerful case, which Smout has subsequently sought to strengthen.[10] The only modern Marxist analysis of Scottish economic development of any substance is even less compromising in its support for an economic interpretation of the Union. Hopes of 'continuing and enhanced accumulation', it was argued, through trade with England and its colonies – along with the security of military and naval protection for trading activities – made Union the 'eminently rational choice' for the Scottish ruling classes.[11]

Challenges

During the later 1970s, however, doubts began to emerge about the significance of economic considerations in accounting for the Union of 1707. At least one historian went to the other extreme and proclaimed boldly that 'the Scots did not enter the union for commercial gain', but argued instead for the primacy of political expediency.[12] As has been noted already, the 'old theory' that the Union was a bargain over trade has been categorised by P. H. Scott as a Victorian 'invention'.[13] The economic argument for union, one of Scott's adherents has declared with delight, 'has been blown out of the water by a generation of political historians who have *researched the archives*' (author's emphasis). The facts, it is asserted, 'speak for themselves', the inference being that as the Union failed to bring a 'dramatic' improvement in Scotland's economic fortunes, it cannot have been entered with this outcome in mind.[14]

Neither of these points need be taken seriously and each is quickly disposed of. First, almost one hundred years before Queen Victoria's reign began, a pamphleteer, possibly Duncan Forbes, reported that although the Union had been carried against 'the Inclinations of the Generality of the People', the 'only popular Topick produced for rendering it palatable, was the great Advantage that must accrue . . . from the Communication of Trade, to which by the Union it [Scotland] was admitted'.[15] As we will see later, this observation can be confirmed by evidence from the period of the Union debate itself. Secondly, that the Union did not produce all that was expected of it (indeed in one writer's view Scotland took *fifty* years to recover from the damage it inflicted) is no argument against the proposition that sufficient numbers of Scots who mattered *believed* in 1706 and 1707 that it would bring economic benefits in its wake. As a matter of fact, however, it is worth pointing out that in *the short term*, many Scottish

landowners, notably those exporting grain and black cattle, benefited enormously from the effects of the Union. Merchants in and
around Glasgow too were able to exploit the opportunities there
were (initially at least by cheating the customs) for extending the
tobacco trade. On the other hand, many types of manufacturing
suffered, as did large sections of the trading community in the east.
Paradoxically, it was this failure of the Union to produce the
anticipated rewards that led to efforts on the part of the Scottish
political leadership, along with Westminster, to *make* the Union work
to Scotland's advantage.[16]

Other historians simply ignore economic considerations, preferring instead to concentrate upon the parts played by faction,
patronage and bribery, as outlined in the previous chapter.
Unsurprisingly, then, even relatively recently the Union has been
colourfully described as the outcome of 'the politics of the closet'.[17]

As will be argued below, such interpretations do not stand up to
close scrutiny. Scott's is based on at least one mistaken assumption and
a blinkered reading of the evidence. The suggestion that, because
some burghs were fearful of the economic impact of the proposed
union, trade was not a factor which attracted support for it, is
unconvincing on two counts: first, it seems to ignore the fact that what
mattered more were the votes of the nobility. As has already been
indicated, members of this class had substantial trading interests. But
even so, albeit by a smallish majority, the burghs too voted in favour,
although more burghs than not agreed that the Convention of Royal
Burghs should petition against. The reasons for burghal opposition
were various, and included the dread of high and crippling levels of
taxation, concern for the Scottish church, and fear of the loss of
Scottish liberties (see Appendix 5). Secondly, and paradoxically, given
Scott's admiration for the arguments and parliamentary endeavours
of Andrew Fletcher, it overlooks the emphasis which Fletcher himself
placed on reaching an agreement with England (although not, to be
sure, in the form of an incorporating union) which would secure
Scotland's economic interests. Trade, Fletcher wrote in 1703, was the
'golden ball' for which all the nations of the world were contending.
It is striking too that from the Hamilton estate papers comes a
memorandum (unfortunately, it is anonymous) on union with

England from the early eighteenth century, in which the writer notes that 'Experience tells us that priest Craft never yet made any Nation either Rich, Wise or Strong'. Law, it was argued, was 'Necessary for Order', but, it was concluded, 'the Hony Lys in the Trade'.[18] Scots, the writer forecast, would, following union, 'screw' into the bowels of the English hive. Another contemporary quoted by Scott (on this occasion to give authoritative support to his view that Scottish acquiescence in 1706 to incorporating union was obtained under the threat of military duress) also gives economic concerns as another reason 'which had greater influence with many'.[19]

At first sight, it might seem that there is a correlation between the specialisms of the various historians concerned, and the degree of emphasis which they placed on economic factors. The time scale being considered is important too. Smout and Mitchison, for instance, are primarily economic (and social) historians, whereas Ferguson, Riley and Cowan concentrated on political issues. However, while this is probably more than a coincidence, speculation along these lines can only be taken so far. For one thing, Smout's interpretation is far from being monocausal. He recognised that, both individually and collectively, members of the Scottish Parliament who voted in favour of the Union did so for several reasons. For another, it was an economic historian, A. M. Carstairs, who, in an important but little-known essay, argued that by 1703 Scotland's long-standing desire for commercial union had *weakened*: the 'communication of trade was still . . . a necessary condition of union, but no longer a powerful inducement'.[20] Fletcher of Saltoun (admittedly no neutral observer) reported something like this in 1703, when he wrote that 'however fond' the Scots had been of a union in the past (he too had earlier been in favour), they were 'now much less concerned for the success of it, from a just sense they have that it would not only prove no remedy for our present condition, but increase the poverty of our country'.[21] The fear was that wealth would be drawn from Scotland to London and that Scottish manufactures would be unable to withstand competition from England. The evidence of growing apprehensions about the economic implications of an incorporating union in the early years of the eighteenth century has been underlined in other quarters too, and will be discussed further below.[22]

Economic historians, however, have tended to take a long view of the Union. Political historians have usually focused upon a shorter period of time. Indeed, it is the work of political historians which has drawn attention to the forces which were holding Scotland and England apart, not the least of which was religion (strident Scottish Presbyterianism as opposed to English Episcopalianism) and the different forms of worship practised in the two countries. It is true too that opposition to the proposed union from the Kirk was a matter of grave concern to men such as the Secretary of State, John Erskine, 11th Earl of Mar. Even after the passing of the Act which sought to preserve the Scottish Church within the context of an incorporating union, fears for its survival in a British (and English-dominated) Parliament featured prominently in anti-union petitions.[23]

Riley's conviction that self-serving political manoeuvring provides the key to 1707 was based in part on his reassessment of economic matters. He too took the view that there was much less enthusiasm for free trade than has commonly been assumed, and pointed out that individuals with particular interests 'were suspicious of economic union'. More importantly, he argued, contrary to what Smout had claimed, religion and not trade dominated the 'pamphlet war' outside Parliament; and he further asserted that controversy about trade was 'a fashionable and convenient camouflage for less respectable motives'.[24] In their private correspondence, politicians made few references to trade; 'self-interested calculation', the maintenance of peace between the two kingdoms, and the need to keep out popery and prevent confusion on the death of the Queen, were the main topics.

Sensibly enough, Riley also argued that the Earl of Roxburghe's oft-quoted 'Trade with most' remarks, made to George Baillie of Jerviswood, should be understood in their proper political context, that is, not as an objective assessment of the situation, but as an attempt by Roxburghe to try to persuade Baillie that he should join the winning side and support incorporating union. It has already been noted that Roxburghe was awarded with a dukedom after 1707. Perhaps Riley's most telling point, however, is that when it came to the crucial votes in 1706, by and large members of the nobility voted according to their current party political alignment and not in accordance with their ostensible economic interests.[25] Where members did have an identifiable economic interest and voted in favour, Riley was persuaded that this was coincidental.

The Economic Case Revisited

The argument that economic interests played a persuasive role in the victory of the pro-unionists has clearly taken a beating. The assault, however, has not been fatal, and in the past two decades new findings and re-assessments of older contributions to the debate have combined to push economic considerations back to centre-stage.

Thus although producing no counter-evidence, Professor Mitchison has sagely, and tellingly, expressed her surprise that modern historians should dismiss the attractions to contemporaries of unhindered trade. If politicians' letters contain few references to the economy, this is hardly surprising, she observes, 'since in all ages a week is a long time in politics', and what mattered to those concerned was what 'could personally be secured in the next few days'.[26] Bigger considerations, in other words, including economic ones, can be taken as read.

Yet the degree to which economic and political spheres were distinct can be exaggerated. Indeed what is often striking in the collections of correspondence of many of the leading magnates is the way in which matters of state and estate jostle together. Thus amongst the Hamilton MSS in the National Archives of Scotland are many letters which show that the Duke of Hamilton was kept constantly aware by his men of business of what was happening on his estates, whether it was proposals for sowing, the condition of the harvest and the success or otherwise of efforts to sell grain, the non-payment of rents, or the fortunes of his coal mines and salt works. The Seafield correspondence contains letters which tell a similar story (Appendix 3). From the regular flow of letters to Edinburgh and London from their chamberlains and factors, most landed proprietors were familiar with the day-to-day business of estate management. It would be remarkable had they not also thought about the prospects for their estate enterprises in the event of a union treaty, even if in some cases these were only a secondary consideration.

The idea, mooted by Riley, that economic issues merely provided 'an element of the language of conflict' is 'extremely difficult to reconcile with the fact that fifteen of the Treaty's twenty-five Articles were unquestionably economic in character.[27] Such records of speeches in Parliament as have survived show that economic subjects were debated, often passionately. It is thus hard to believe that most speakers who referred to trade did not actually mean what they said. And there are reasons to believe that they did, at least according to the paraphrased speeches generated by Sir John Clerk from his diary and other notes.[28] Such a conclusion finds support in the voting patterns in the Scottish Parliament in 1706 which, according to Allan Macinnes, show that the 'most keenly contested issues were . . . economic'.[29]

Recent research on this topic, however, has moved away from the idea that the Scots saw union *only* as an opportunity to enter a 'common market' with England and her growing colonial empire, the final working out of forces which had been drawing the two countries closer together for over a century. It is rather more complicated than that; grand generalisations about 'Scotland's' motives for supporting union read well,[30] but obscure the rather more complex – and in many respects more prosaic – reality of a mixed bag of motives. Scotsmen in 1705 and 1706 did not yearn for the return of a Cromwellian golden age. Nor were their rationally based economic aspirations uniform.

It has been argued that 'the whole grubby parliamentary drama was fought out against the backcloth of English threats to Scottish trade'.[31] By far the most intimidating of these was the English Aliens Act of 1705, which has been aptly described by Professor Bruce Lenman as a 'formidable economic bludgeon'. Passed at Westminster in March 1705, it was to come into effect if the Scots had not entered into negotiations for a treaty of union (or accepted the Hanoverian succession) by Christmas Day. It had the desired effect. As Smout observed, Scotland needed England and English markets which were already open, never mind new ones. This is potently demonstrated by a single statistic: in 1703 black cattle sales accounted for something like 40 per cent of all Scottish exports to England. This played a crucial part in maintaining a favourable trade balance and was therefore necessary for Scottish survival, as too were the revenues from sales to the estates on which they were reared and the incomes of the drovers. So too were sales of linen cloth, the only other trading commodity the value of sales of which rivalled (and in some years overtook) black cattle before 1707.

What the disastrous experience of Darien had shown was the brutal fact that if the Scots were to trade overseas successfully, they required English acquiescence, and access to her colonies. English investment had been withdrawn from the Company of Scotland after the English East India Company had pressured King William on this point and persuaded him to take their part against Scottish interests. One reason for the failure of a relief expedition to Darien in 1699 was the refusal by the English to supply the Scots with provisions in the West Indies. Resentment thus grew at the way Scotland's interests were either ignored or adversely affected by English foreign policy decisions. The Union of the Crowns had effectively removed Scotland's right to take independent action. Reference has been made to England's wars with France between 1689 and 1697 and from 1702, which exacerbated Scotland's mounting economic problems, and had a devastating effect on the trade, prosperity and population of a west-coast burgh such as Ayr, which was engaged more heavily than most in the importation of French wines.[32]

It has been suggested by one eminent historian that the difficulties of the 1690s were 'essentially temporary', and had little bearing on the causes of the Union of 1707.[33] Yet the troubles which the Scottish economy had begun to experience in the later 1680s were not relieved until the 1730s and 1740s. The upturn which can be discerned in 1705 was faint and unsustained, and simply took Scotland off the bottom of the trough of 1704, when the deficit on Scottish visible trade may have been in the region of £2 million Scots.[34] Scottish linen sales abroad were faltering, and indeed imports of linen, muslin and cotton were more valuable than exports of what was lower-grade cloth. Conflict between English and Scottish trading interests became more intense in the early 1700s. Recently published research in this area has shown that the periodic seizure of Scottish vessels and incarceration of their crews had been a feature of Anglo-Scottish maritime relations since 1688, culminating in a rare (but well-known) retaliatory measure taken by the Scots, the capture at Leith by agents of the Company of

Scotland of the English vessel, the *Worcester*, and the hanging of some of her officers. It was a desperate act on the part of a Scottish population which was acutely aware – and resentful – of English domination at sea. This fact pressed harder on the authorities on both sides of the Border the need for the resolution of tensions between the two countries.[35] Wartime privateering was hitting the Scots hard too: Bo'ness for example, through which much of Glasgow's overseas trade was conducted, claimed that only a third of the ships sailing from the port in 1698 were there in 1705, while of 557 resident families, 205 were those of widows.[36]

Furthermore, despite the advances which had been made during the seventeenth century, in agriculture and commerce, tax-gathering methods were lax and Scotland's national finances were in such a poor condition pre-1707 that there was insufficient revenue to pay for the army, civil establishment and government. In short, according to virtually the sole authority on the Scottish Exchequer, 'an independent Scotland was not financially viable',[37] and unable to fully fund either the military or civil service. As was observed in the previous chapter, one of the uses to which the Equivalent was put was the payment of Scotland's public debts stretching back to at least 1702, not only in the form of fees, salaries and pensions for the better-off, but also lesser individuals, such as John Murray, a gunner at Fort William, who had been owed £10. As will be seen below, the penuriousness of the Scottish government had implications for the maintenance of order, with some politicians being acutely aware that the military was under-armed and that the potential consequences of this in the event of serious physical opposition to the proposed union could have dire consequences. Nor was the position improving, or nearly as buoyant as some historians have suggested. There is no doubt that Scotland's economy had made considerable progress during the course of the seventeenth century, but even in agriculture there are indications that all may not have been well beneath the surface (and beyond the confines of proprietors' policies and home farms) towards the end of the century. Nitrogen levels were falling, for example, with deleterious effects on crop levels, and were only replenished in privileged localities where liming was practised. It was little wonder, then, that there was an exodus of Scottish farmers to Ulster.[38]

Scotland's financial weakness and as a consequence her vulnerabil-
ity beyond her own coastline can readily be demonstrated: in 1695, in
order to defend her shipping against French privateers, the Scots had
to go cap in hand to the English to lend them naval hulls, although the
fitting out and running costs were to be paid for by the Scottish
Exchequer. Scotland's pre-1707 navy comprised some two frigates.
The Scottish Parliament was thus confronted with the harsh reality of
Scotland's economic weakness – as well as what has been described as
a form of economic blackmail – and had virtually no choice but to
discuss union on English terms. Scotsmen were learning the hard way
that without political control over its export markets, Scotland was
simply unable to survive in an age of growing economic nationalism:
'mercantilism in a time of stagnation is a weapon that can only be
employed successfully by the fairly strong'.[39] Mercantilist solutions
to Scotland's widely perceived economic problems – relative poverty,
unemployment and economic backwardness – were strongly canvassed
from around 1700. Indeed the growth of interest in economic matters
in Scotland is revealed by the eightfold increase in the numbers of
books published on political economy in Scotland between the 1660s
and the end of the century. After Darien, and a series of other largely
unsuccessful measures instituted by the Scottish Parliament and Privy
Council with the aim of developing the country's manufacturing
sector, the future of an independent Scottish economy looked bleak.
With less than a handful of exceptions, all of Scotland's state-
supported manufacturing projects had run into the sand.

The suggestion has been made by T. M. Devine that the failure of
Scottish mercantilist policies was unimportant as far as the Union was
concerned.[40] On the contrary, it was just this unpalatable fact that
persuaded some leading members of Scottish society – who were
'thinking like men in England, France, Holland and Germany' – to
consider seriously Scotland's options. It is within this realistic but more
optimistic and forward-looking context that Union should be understood. The claim that it was only Seton of Pitmedden who argued
along these lines (because he was in the pay of the government) is at
best mischievous and, at worst, betrays a singular ability to ignore
great wads of evidence which point in a very different direction.[41]

An example of this sort of thinking in practice is provided by Sir

John Clerk of Penicuik, who, as we have seen, was also conscious that the English might resort to a military solution if a negotiated settlement about the succession could not be reached. In Clerk's view, however, what had a greater influence on some Scottish members was 'the prohibition of our black cattle in England . . . and (which was worse) a moral certainty that England wou'd never allow us to grou rich and powerfull in a separate state'. The testimony of Clerk, a reluctant unionist who was evidently persuaded to become a union Commissioner only after the Duke of Queensberry threatened to 'withdraw all friendship' (a euphemism for patronage), is confirmed in a letter sent by the burgh of Montrose to their parliamentary representative, James Scott, in October 1706.

Although the burgh council declared that the advantages of incorporating union were 'many and great', the main thrust of their argument was that if the Aliens Act or anything like it was to be enforced, the merchants of Montrose 'would be deprived of the only valuable branch of our trade [linen cloth]', without which the 'fate of this poor miserable blinded nation' could easily be foretold.[42] In fact, despite its initial optimism, this document helps to confirm the suspicions of those historians who have argued that if the Scottish burghs had been convinced of the economic advantages of union, they would have welcomed it with open arms. Instead, as has been noted already, inside Parliament they were considerably less enthusiastic than the nobility. Outside, the burghs (although not all of them) were prominent campaigners against the Articles. The document referred to here substantiates the view that the Scots 'did not go into the union simply because they were poor and saw no other way of riches, but because they were poor and getting poorer'.[43] But Clerk's *History* makes it clear that both Clerk himself, and other Scottish political figures, did not support the Union solely for negative economic reasons. Looking back from the vantage point of 1744, Clerk reflected that prior to 1707, while he had been conscious that England, 'by the strength & number of her Ships of War had a just claime to the Sovereignty of the seas', he was 'a stranger to the Sovereignty of Scotland, except within her own confines'.[44] 'Independency', he continued, was a 'meer shadow', but one nevertheless which many Scots appeared to wish to remain sheltered behind.

Downsitting of the Scottish Estates (Parliament), c.1680. The engraving shows the procession of parliamentarians, officials and others from Holyrood to Parliament House. At the top, in the centre, is the Royal Throne, seat of the King's Commissioner. Near the front of the procession are the county, burgh and town commissioners (members of Parliament). *National Museums of Scotland.*

Gesso panel depicting a Royal review of the British fleet, c.1708. One of the major benefits of the Union for Scotland was the protection of convoys of merchant ships which was provided by the Royal Navy. An important pre-1707 weakness of the Scots merchants was the small size and powerlessness of their navy. *National Museums of Scotland.*

Queen Anne (1665-1714), by W. Lissing. Like her predecessor later in life, William
Orange, Queen Anne was an ardent pro-unionist. The death of her final survivi
child in 1700, which left the succession in doubt, concentrated English attention
Scottish attitudes to the British monarchy. *Scottish National Portrait Gallery.*

Sir James Douglas, 2nd Duke of Queensberry (1662-1711), by an unknown artist. Known as the 'Union Duke', Queensberry was disliked by Queen Anne, but his management of the Scottish Parliament was crucial. With his supporters such as the Earl of Mar, and his many dependents (as well as Squadrone or 'new party' votes), he successfully steered the Articles of Union through Parliament during the final months of 1706. Well rewarded for his efforts. *Scottish National Portrait Gallery.*

Sir John Clerk of Penicuik (1676-1755), by an unknown artist. Clerk was one of th
Union Commissioners appointed by Queen Anne in 1705. Scottish patriot and poly
math. A reluctant supporter of incorporating union, and troubled thereafter that h
had voted in favour, but Clerk was a realist. *Scottish National Portrait Gallery.*

Anne, Duchess of Hamilton (1632-1716), mother of James, 4th Duke of Hamilton (1658-1712). Anne was firmly anti-unionist, in which cause she was active. Nominally James was too, although his erratic behaviour and betrayal of the opposition at crucial moments disappointed both his mother and his supporters. *The Hamilton Collection, Lennoxlove.*

THE
Lord *Beilhaven*'s Speech
IN
PARLIAMENT
The Second day of November 1706.
ON THE

Subject-Matter of an Union *betwixt the Two Kingdoms of* Scotland *and* England.

My Lord Chancellor,

WHEN I confider this Affair of an UNION betwixt the Two Nations, as it is expref's'd in the feveral *Articles* there of, and now the Subject of our Deliberation at this time; I find my Mind crowded with variety of very Melancholy Thoughts, and I think it my Duty to disburden my felf of fome of them, by laying them before, and expofing them to the ferious Confideration of this Honourable Houfe.

I think, I fee *a Free and Independent Kingdom* delivering up That, which all the World hath been Fighting for, fince the days of *Nimrod*; yea, That for which moft of all the Empires, Kingdoms, States, Principalities and Dukedoms of *Europe*, are at this very time engaged in the moft Bloody and Cruel Wars that ever were, *to wit,* A Power to Manage their own Affairs by themfelves, without the Affiftance and Counfel of any other.

I think, I fee *a National Church,* founded upon a Rock, fecured by a *Claim of Right,* hedged and fenced about by the ftricteft and pointedeft Legal Sanction that Sovereignty could contrive, voluntarily defcending into a Plain, upon an equal Level with *Jews, Papifts, Socinians, Arminians, Anabaptifts,* and other Sectaries, *&c.*

A   1

Lord Belhaven's Speech in Parliament, 2 November 1706. John Hamilton (1656–1708), 2nd Lord Belhaven, was a Williamite turned Jacobite. Like Clerk, he was a patriot, but Belhaven was passionately anti-union, fearing the loss of Scotland's independence. This expressive speech, which began with Belhaven's statement that his mind was 'crowded with a variety of very Melancholy Thoughts', was one of several popular speeches which were printed and circulated outside Parliament House. *National Museums of Scotland.*

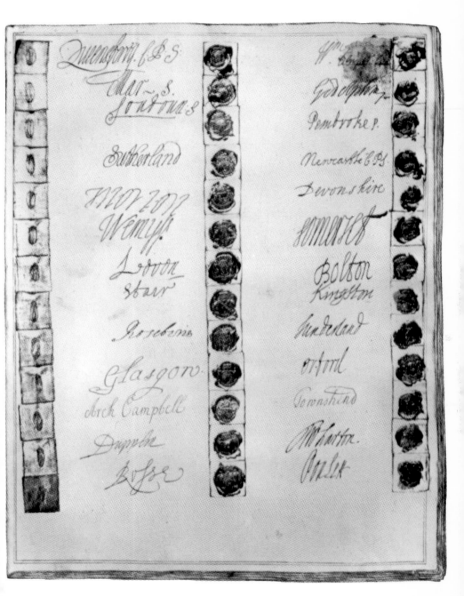

Signatories to the Articles of Union, 22 July 1706. The signatures are of the Commissioners from England and Scotland who met to formulate the conditions upon which the proposed union was to be settled. From the outset it was made clear that England's representatives would only discuss incorporating union. The list is headed on the Scottish side by the Duke of Queensberry and on England's by William Cowper. *National Archives of Scotland.*

Standard English quart wine measure, Stirling, 1 May 1707. The XVIIth Article of Union had declared that from 1 May 1707 Scottish weights and measures were to be 'as are established in England', enforced by the burghs. It was an unpopular imposition, and Scottish weights and measures continued to be used for several decades. *National Museums of Scotland.*

If a significant number of Scots parliamentarians were not also persuaded of the more positive aspects of free trade, it is hard to understand why the IVth Article of Union, which provided for 'full Freedom and Intercourse of Trade and Navigation', was so strongly supported. There were only nineteen votes against, while twenty-six otherwise 'consistent ' opponents of union breached party lines and voted in favour. Clearly this was a major relief for all those connected with the linen and black cattle trades. It can reasonably be argued too that the vote for this Article represented the cross-party support there was for an aspiration to which many Scots had been wedded since the prospect of free trade had first been laid invitingly in front of them by James VI. At first sight too, it appears to substantiate the determinist case, and provides support for those who have argued that this was a victory for the Scots' 'ruling oligarchy', who sought through union to 'galvanize the nation into economic improvement'.[45] To conclude thus, however, would be to over simplify. It is an argument too which depends overmuch on hindsight.

The View from England (and Ireland)

What has been ignored until recently is that the granting of free trade to the Scots required a change in *English* attitudes. A proposal for parliamentary union which had been commended by King William in 1689, for example, was largely ignored at Westminster, and even after the same monarch's plea for a 'firm and entire Union' just eight days prior to his death in 1702, and his successor Queen Anne's even stronger support for a similar move, interest in a closer relationship with Scotland within Parliament ebbed and flowed with changing Whig (and Tory) appreciations of what political advantage they could gain from it. The renewal of hostilities with France in 1702 concentrated minds elsewhere in the short term. What appears to have been the dominant Tory view was expressed in 1700 by their leader in the House of Commons, Sir Edward Seymour, who remarked contemptuously that union with Scotland would be like marrying a beggar, and that 'whoever married a beggar could only expect a louse for her portion'. Yet this was not a new attitude. It had its roots in the Elizabethan era. English interest in Scotland was certainly not inspired by the prospect of economic gain, despite the efforts of the Earl of Cromartie to persuade English consumers of the benefits of cheap goods.[46] Nevertheless, in the early eighteenth century there was a weakening of what had hitherto been powerful opposition from English merchants and manufacturers to commercial union, which had been based on largely unwarranted fears of Scottish competition.[47] As a result of the temporary shift in opinion, English union negotiators after 1705 found themselves in a position where they could grant what have been described as 'remarkable' concessions to the Scots, not only the IVth Article, but also subsidies for Scottish products and preferential rates of taxation.[48] These were crucially important gains to the Scots, but are invariably overlooked by historians intent on stressing English bullying.

Although these concessions were often granted grudgingly, so substantial were they that they produced a wail of protest from Ireland, 'John Bull's Other Kingdom', which in 1703 had petitioned Queen Anne for union. Weekly, the *Dublin Gazette* published in envious detail the prizes obtained by the Scots. In a short tract written early in 1707 (but not published until after his death) Jonathan Swift railed against the 'stinking' and perfidious Scots who had obtained a favourable union settlement with England, which had ignored Ireland's loyalty and superior claims to such an arrangement.

Also worthy of note is what some historians see as the concession over Scottish representation in the House of Commons: the English commissioners had in June 1706 initially proposed that the Scots should have 38 MPs. Following Scottish representations (for at least 50), this was raised, with little resistance, to 45, even though this was more than was justified by the tax ratio between the two countries (around 38:1 in England's favour), but not sufficient if population was to be used as the basis of representation, although this was not a serious consideration at the time. It should be borne in mind, however, as wary opponents of the proposal to grant the Scots so many seats did, that provided most Scottish MPs could be persuaded to act at Westminster in the Whig junto interest, their numbers did not matter. Indeed, within limits, the more the merrier.[49]

However, the critical factor which both confirmed English Whig interest in an incorporating union, and gave the Scots better economic terms than had been available during the unsuccessful union negotiations in 1702–3, was the continuing conflict with France, during the War of the Spanish Succession. In terms of manpower, this was the most demanding war in which England had been involved. In addition to an army of some 120,000 men between 1706 and 1711, and a navy 43,000 strong, the number of royal naval vessels rose from roughly 160 in 1688 to around 225 in 1714. The financial resources required to pay for this were unprecedentedly hefty, totalling £140 million for the wars against France between 1689 and 1713.

England was a strongly emerging fiscal-military state, battling with France over the supremacy of continental Europe. With the capture of Gibralter in 1704, followed by military victories at Blenheim, also in 1704 and Ramillies in 1706, England was clearly in the ascendant. But in 1705/6 England had not yet reached Great Power status. Military defeats were to be experienced in Spain. Victory in Europe was not yet assured.

The Scottish Parliament, however, was displaying a new-found independence and, indeed, as has been seen, had in 1703 openly defied Queen Anne by passing the Act of Security and the Act anent Peace and War. It was just conceivable that under the growing influence of disgruntled Episcopalians, the Scots, increasingly ungovernable, might have revived the 'auld alliance' with France in the hope of restoring the House of Stuart. Scottish troops might conceivably be withdrawn at this critical juncture from the European theatre. The war against Louis XIV was much less popular in Scotland, which had in effect been hijacked into the conflict.[50] Such fears were heightened by reports that arms and munitions were being shipped in France for Scotland.[51]

Scotland therefore had to be contained. Although a military solution was an option, and might be (and was, indirectly) threatened, prudence and Whig ambitions at Westminster (see above) made incorporating union (as opposed to the uncertainty for the Hanoverian succession of a federal union) the better choice. This secured control of Scottish politicians who would henceforth be Westminster-based and, more important, made sure of the Hanoverian Succession and the security of England's border with Scotland. The Protestant Succession, it should be emphasised, and the peace of Britain, were in the interests of many Scots too.

Supply-side Weaknesses and the 'Explanations'

Where the received economic argument falls down is in its assumption that Scottish economic interests lay wholly in the direction of English markets. This is a *demand-side* analysis, which assumes that Scotland's economic problem was seen to be simply inadequate demand. It ignores the very real *supply-side* weaknesses which were apparent virtually throughout the whole of the Scottish economy. Some of these have already been referred to. The problem was not only that there had been temporary setbacks, and that market opportunities were restricted, but that such economic progress as had been taking place in the second half of the seventeenth century was based upon precarious foundations. Whatever Scotland's undoubted underlying economic potential, it was far from being realised around 1700. Necessary structural changes in agriculture, for example, remained in the future, while Scotland lagged behind Ireland in terms of the size and adaptability of its market sector. Scottish products such as woollen cloth were of a poor quality and increasingly difficult to sell outside Scotland; the finer the cloth, the more easily it succumbed to English competition. The paper industry faced similar problems.[52]

Consequently, it has been argued that, although a majority of those Scots involved in the making of the Treaty clearly grasped the opportunity of access to English and colonial markets while it was on offer, others were equally concerned to obtain as many safeguards as possible to *defend* vulnerable elements of what was an exceedingly fragile economy.[53]

This is in keeping with the suggestions noted already that commercial interests in Scotland were much more cautious about union in the early 1700s than had been the case earlier. Certainly 'Scottish requests were made [by the union Commissioners] in more detail and with far greater precision than in the previous negotiations'[54] At a time of rampant mercantilism throughout Europe, in their economic thinking the Scots were 'severely practical'.[55]

It may be that as the potentially damaging consequences of English pressure in November 1705 for incorporating union began to be foreseen, those who were threatened did their utmost to add what flesh they could to the bare bones of the treaty then on offer. It should be noted that in the months before September 1705 when the vote was taken which committed the Scots to discussion of a treaty of union with England, and up to the appointment in April 1706 by the Queen of the Scottish Commissioners who were to negotiate a union (and who were presented immediately with English insistence that only an incorporating union was acceptable), there was much discussion in the Scottish Parliament about the condition of Scotland's trade. Indeed there were hopes as late as August that something could be done to limit English discrimination against Scottish exports, and in September, as the 1705 session of Parliament drew to a close, a Scottish Council of Trade was set up. In November 1705 even the usually well-informed Earl of Seafield, the Lord Chancellor, who 'functioned [on behalf of the Court] as a permanent civil servant with Scotland as his "department"', seemed unsure whether the treaty negotiations were to be about the succession or a union.[56] Thus it was only at the beginning of 1706 that it became obvious that some form of federal treaty was out of the question, and that Scotland would lose all control over its economic policy.

Support for this proposition is to be found within the Articles of Union themselves. Too rarely studied are those versions of the Articles which show which of them were amended as a result of Scottish demands.

Articles X–XIII relieved Scottish-made paper, windows and malt, as well as coal, culm and cinders, from English duties for varying periods of time. The fiscal concessions were to last only for the duration of the war, but that they were applied to the commodities as they were can reasonably be interpreted as the outcome of special pleading. Those most concerned were anxious to retain the home market in Scotland, which they feared was vulnerable to English incursions. Under the terms of the XIIth Article the coal proprietors along the banks of the River Forth and its estuary managed to obtain relief from coastal duties on coal. As a result, they were sheltered from competition from Tyneside within the estuarial limits of the Forth, which contained two of Scotland's three most densest concentrations of population, including Edinburgh. Neither the salt nor the coal proprietors showed any interest in sales beyond Scotland, other than exceptionally. The claim that 'by 1706 at least, the protectionists seem to have lost the initiative'[57] is simply without substance. A similar judgement may be passed on the linked propositions that the Treaty of Union was 'not a bargain of any kind' and that the negotiations were 'fake'.[58] The Scottish economy was indeed weak and vulnerable, but numbers of Scots parliamentarians, and those who had access to them, fought tenaciously to defend what parts of it they could.

The Articles relating to trade and taxation were debated and amended in the Scottish Parliament during November and December 1706. This stage of the parliamentary proceedings, the so-called 'Explanations', has attracted little interest on the part of historians. Contemporaries, however, treated them rather more seriously. Daniel Defoe, for instance, remarked that the consequences of denying the additional drawbacks and bounties demanded by the Scots would have been 'Very Great'.[59] So heated did the debate over Scottish exemptions from English salt taxes (in the VIIIth Article) become that he described this Article as the 'Grand Affair'. On 12 December, the eve of the debate, the Earl of Mar told Sir David Nairne, Deputy-Secretary in London for Scottish affairs, that this was 'the artickle I was most afraid of'. Unless alterations to it were made, there was a danger not only that the Court would be defeated, but that this would lead to further routs and indeed threaten the whole treaty.[60] Significantly, it was over the question of salt duties that the Court suffered a rare defeat, with the opposition forces winning on 20 December 1706 by a single vote. It is difficult to reconcile the apparent seriousness of this situation with Riley's comment that a 'disproportionate' amount of time was spent discussing the salt question. What the Article did was protect the Scottish salt masters from foreign competition in the home market (thus continuing Scottish policy), and ensure too that Scottish consumers would pay a lower price for salt – an essential element in the diet of the poor as well as the rich – than would otherwise have been the case.

A number of possible reasons have been given for the passions – and extremely close voting – which marked this stage in the proceedings: excitement; a 'final gesture of independence by some members of the Scottish parliament', who tried to wreck the treaty by making demands which the English Parliament would be bound to refuse; and a political tactic on the part of the Court to 'indicate that they were not as dependent on the English as they might have appeared'.[61] Each of these has some merit. The problem is that not one of the possibilities reported here is grounded on hard evidence.

This does exist, however, in the form of the correspondence between the Earl of Mar and Sir David Nairne. Largely on the basis of this, an alternative interpretation can be advanced. Riley and others failed to appreciate the significance to contemporaries of the importance of commodities such as malt, salt and coal, and the consequences for prices and employment of a common, British, tax regime. Mar's letters provide few grounds for believing anything other than that while there were exceptions, by and large, opposition to the unamended Articles is to be explained largely in terms of the subjects with which the Articles themselves were concerned (Appendix 4).

There were real fears that taxation, levied at English rates, would be profoundly damaging to Scottish trade. The recently unearthed petition from the burgh of Stirling best expresses this in predicting that union would 'bring ane Insupportable burden of Taxatione upon this Land, which all the Grant of freedome of Trade will never Counterballance being so uncertain and precarious' (Appendix 5).[62] The point was also made that they would be without 'any parliament to hear & help us Except that of a British one'.

While the Court could do nothing to alter this, as has been seen, steps were taken to try to disarm the critics. Indeed, although reluctantly, the Court had no choice but to 'take all the ways [possible] . . . to satisfy people'. Thus the future of the Scottish Church, another concern of some of the burghs, was secured in a separate Act, passed on 12 November. This had resulted from Presbyterian fears that unless guarded in this way, the Church of Scotland, against the will of its adherents, might later be absorbed by the Church of England. From this point onwards, moderate Presbyterians, led by the Williamite and politically shrewd Rev. William Carstares, urged ministers and presbyteries to cease campaigning against incorporation.[63] Not all responded, and in the south-west, Covenanting opposition to the proposed union with Scotland's sinful southern neighbour was maintained.

Favourable amendments were made to several of the proposed levels of excise duties and drawbacks. Such changes, it should be emphasised, were in direct conflict with the principles of free trade and equal taxation, which were enshrined in the IVth and VIth Articles respectively. It is worth considering that these measures may have been sufficient to persuade a small majority of burgh representatives that in the light of the potential losses to trade otherwise, they should vote in favour of union. Obviously, by no means all of the burghs were convinced, but this may have been because they were interested in more than trade.

Most of the amendments would have further warmed the landowners to the idea of incorporating union. Coal and salt have already been mentioned. In another amendment, several private rights, usually of exemptions from customs and excise duties granted by the Scottish Parliament and Privy Council, were to 'remain safe and entire' for those to whom they applied. A notable beneficiary was Sir Peter Halkett of Pitfirrane, a member of the Squadrone Volante, whose coal was largely unsaleable in Scotland. Halkett, who represented the burgh of Dunfermline in Parliament, rejected his constituents' plea to vote against the union, allegedly because 'he had been threatened by those in high power, the granters of privileges, that if he did not . . . his coal privileges would not be renewed'.[64] Landowners also benefited further from the insertion of a clause which guaranteed their right to drive black cattle over the Border into England duty-free, and by a drawback on oatmeal exports, conceded after sustained pressure on their behalf. Mar expressed the hope that the amendment would 'not be thought inconsistent with the Treaty'. As it happens, this measure was enormously successful for those east-coast landowners who were in a position to benefit from it. Ironically, it also produced bitter social conflict in 1720, part of a wider pattern of disturbance resulting from the Union, which contributed to the pressure to repeal it or make it meet better the needs of Scotland.[65] The current prohibition on grain imported from Ireland was also to be continued.

It was not landowners alone, however, either individually or as a class, whose interests were looked after. £2,000 per annum from the Equivalent was laid aside for 'encouraging and promoting the

Manufacture of Coarse Wool', the view being taken that this would not present any danger to England, as Scottish wool was tarred. Because some of the woolmasters 'wou'd have been very troublesome otherwise', Mar decided that the easiest course would be to accede to their demand.[66]

In short, while several of the amendments to the Articles would have a broad impact, many of the economic favours which were granted by the Court to both individuals and sectional interests may reasonably be interpreted as means of sugaring the pill of incorporating union, and can comfortably be set alongside the better-known forms of political management and bribery referred to earlier. Towards the end of 1706, and under the sort of close scrutiny which results when economic theory is turned into practice, access to English markets looked 'a lot less like the panacea for Scotland's economic ills' than it had done earlier. The amendments gave to the final Treaty a pragmatic quality which reflects the fact that not only politically, but also in the economic sphere, the opportunities sought were often for the economic advancement of Scotsmen rather than for the economic growth of Scotland, although the last was probably more deeply considered than is sometimes supposed. Not surprisingly perhaps, Sir John Clerk wanted to emphasise the selflessness of the union Commissioners, reporting that 'no private interests whatever' interfered 'with those of the nation'. It was to 'earn the thanks of posterity', not of the mob, that the unionists had borne the jibes and odium which were heaped on their shoulders.[67]

Extra-Parliamentary Pressure

One factor which has been noted by virtually every historian who has written about the Union is the strength of public feeling against it. Only one dissenting voice of any note has been heard,[68] although others have attempted to minimise the extent of opposition, least legitimately by means of the reductive device of mild sarcasm.[69]

Although the proposition that it 'is always easier to raise a petition of protest than one of approval' may partly explain the apparent absence of popular sympathy for the Union, the fact is that attempts to generate public support in favour failed abysmally. Yet on other occasions in early-modern Scotland, crowds could be mobilised in support of pro-establishment, élite-led demonstrations where the purpose was a popular one.

What is undeniable is that while most of the burghs and shires in Scotland did not petition, all of the petitions which were sent (including the recently discovered one sent to the Duke of Hamilton by the pupils of the High School in Edinburgh's Canongate) were opposed to the proposed union for one reason or another. Addresses against the proposed union were signed in and around Stirling, with opposition coming not only from the ranks of the barons and freeholders. Parishes too protested, with heads of families signing in some places late in November and even December, thereby indicating that rank-and-file Presbyterianism had not been entirely satisfied by the separate Act of 12 November which had secured the Scottish Church.[70] Anti-Union demonstrations were commonplace in Edinburgh from the middle of October and, in a number of Scottish towns, notably Dumfries, Kirkcudbright and Stirling, the Articles were publicly burnt by crowds which seem to have had a mind of their own. Lanarkshire was a particularly hot troublespot, with clear evidence that an armed rising and march on Edinburgh were planned, as well as from the Atholl lands. In Edinburgh and at Whitehall, there was deep anxiety about what was happening in the country.

Recent research has shown that the extent of dissent within Scottish society was greater in the first post-Union decades than was apparent to previous historians, and that far from being an 'utter flop', the Jacobite conspiracy of 1708 was built upon much more substantial foundations – of popular opposition to the Union – than was formerly believed.[71] There is an unconfirmed claim that as many as 200 anti-union clubs were formed after 1702, while only one, the Duke of Queensberry's Union club, appears to have been set up in support of incorporation.[72]

What has not been explored, however, is the impact of popular opinion on the members of the Scottish Parliament. The tendency has been to disregard it and focus on the activities of the political élite in isolation. What has been observed is that while some members of Parliament were inclined to be dismissive of crowds of angry demonstrators, such was the general level of concern that the vote late in October 1706 on the proclamation which outlawed 'seditious' meetings was one of the few which resulted in an absolute majority for the Court.[73] Indeed the level of popular disorder outside Parliament in the autumn of 1706 was such that pro-unionists in London began to take note of it. On 1 November 1706 Godolphin wrote that:

The mobb is uneasy at the Union in Scotland, and has been very unruly. The majority in the Parliament is so great, that they begin to find it cannot bee resisted but by tumult and open force. What effect this may have I doe not know, but I hope they won't prove the strongest.[7]

Much anger was directed towards Sir Patrick Johnston, one of the MPs for Edinburgh who had also been a union Commissioner. Accordingly, and following requests from Scotland, troops were moved closer to the Scottish border in England and further north in Ireland, where five regiments, three of horse, and one each of foot and dragoons, were ready for embarkation across the Irish Sea. Efforts too were made to placate extra-parliamentary forces through assurances that their civil and religious concerns would be looked after.

Analysis of London crowds in both the Restoration and early Hanoverian eras has shown that the 'mob' was not only politically aware and had a voice, but also that it was 'a much more positive force in politics' than is usually thought. The crowd played a part in the culture and government of towns and indeed states in the pre-democratic age which historians ignore at their peril.[75] In relation to Scotland, it is a subject which has already begun to repay closer investigation.[76]

In 1706 the tradesmen in Glasgow, for instance, were sufficiently sophisticated to declare their opposition to *incorporating* union rather than simply to union with England. A cursory glance at the printed sources available suggests that the extra-parliamentary crowd played at least some part in determining the final shape of the Articles of Union. Daniel Defoe, who was convinced that the Scottish 'rabble' was the 'worst of its kind', reported to Harley in December 1706, as troops were being marched to Glasgow to restore order, that 'these Tumults and Terrors have brought all the Mischiefs on and tis

Impossible to Avoid the Amendments'. This was a view shared by the Earl of Mar, who, though reluctant to amend the Articles (partly through fear that these would then be rejected in England), was acutely aware of the weak position the authorities in Scotland would be in should a 'commotion' arise, and that therefore some concessions to popular opinion would have to be made. With a number of members of Parliament deciding to 'satisfy the generality of the country' by pressing for amendments, the Court had little choice but to concede. If Parliament was adjourned, the likelihood was that on its return, the fragile pro-Union majority would have disappeared.

Accordingly, partly because of crowd pressure, excise duties on ale, malt and salt were reduced, the first with the assistance of Daniel Defoe, with the result that there was a measurable drop in the level of extra-parliamentary opposition. Until further research is done, it will only be possible to speculate what might have happened had the concessions not been made. One possibility is that English troops would have been marched into Scotland. That concessions were granted, both because of pressure from outside and inside Parliament, may well have finally secured the Union peaceably.

NOTES TO CHAPTER 3

1. G. M. Trevelyan, *Ramillies and the Union with Scotland*, 180; G. S. Pryde, *Scotland from 1603 to the Present Day* (London, 1962), 54.
2. Quoted in P. H. Scott, *1707: The Union of Scotland and England* (Edinburgh, 1979), 27.
3. T. C. Smout, *Scottish Trade on the Eve of Union, 1660–1707* (Edinburgh, 1979), 261–70.
4. J. MacKinnon, *The Union of England and Scotland: A Study in International History* (London, 1896), 227; Mathieson, *Scotland and the Union: A History of Scotland from 1645 to 1747* (Glasgow, 1905), 146.
5. D. Daiches (ed.), *Fletcher of Saltoun: Selected Writings* (Edinburgh, 1979), xxvi.
6. Smout, *Scottish Trade*, 238, 458.

7. Ibid., 462–6.

8. Quoted in R. Mitchison, *Lordship to Patronage: Scotland, 1603–1745* (London, 1983), 135, and see Appendix 1.

9. Smout, *Scottish Trade*, 229–32, 272.

10. T. C. Smout, 'The Burgh of Montrose and the Union of 1707 – a document', *Scottish Historical Review*, LXVI (October, 1987), 183–4.

11. D. Dickson (ed), *Scottish Capitalism: Class, State and Nation from before the Union to the Present* (London, 1980), 86–7.

12. Cowan, 'The Inevitability of Union – A Historical Fallacy?', *Scotia*, V (1991), 6.

13. P. H. Scott, 'Why Did the Scots Accept the Union', *Scottish Affairs*, 1 (Autumn, 1992), 125; see too P. H. Scott, '*The Boasted Advantages': The Consequences of the Union of 1707* (Edinburgh, 1999), 21–3.

14. R. Finlay, 'Caledonia or north Britain? Scottish Identity in the Eighteenth Century', in D. Broun, R. J. Finlay and M. Lynch (eds.), *Image and Identity: The Making and Re-Making of Scotland Through the Ages* (Edinburgh, 1998), 145; a similar point is made by J. R. Young, 'The Parliamentary Incorporating Union of 1707: Political Management, Anti-Unionism and Foreign Policy', in T. M. Devine and J. R. Young (eds.), *Eighteenth Century Scotland: New Perspectives* (East Linton, 1999), 25.

15. D. Forbes (?), *Some Considerations On the Present State of Scotland in a Letter to the Commissioners and Trustees for Improving the Fisheries and Manufactures* (1744), 4.

16. This argument is developed at length in Whatley, *Scottish Society, 1707–1830: Beyond Jacobitism, Towards Industrialisation* (Manchester, 2000), chapters 1–4.

17. Kidd, *Subverting Scotland's Past: Scottish Whig Historians and the Creation of an Anglo-British Identity, 1689–c.1830* (Cambridge, 1993), 50. This is the only flaw in an otherwise superb – and important – book.

18. Quoted in C. A. Whatley, 'Bought and sold for English gold? The debate about the causes of the Union of 1707 clarified', in R. Jackson and S. Wood (eds.), *Images of Scotland* (Dundee, 1997), 33.

19. P. H. Scott, *Andrew Fletcher and the Treaty of the Union* (Edinburgh, 1992), 169.

20. A. M. Carstairs, 'Some Economic Aspects of the Union of the Parliaments', *Scottish Journal of Political Economy*, 2 (1955), 65–7.

21. Daiches, *Fletcher of Saltoun*, 117.

22. B. P. Levack, *The Formation of the British State* (Oxford, 1987), 149–52.

23. See D. Defoe, *The History of the Union of Great Britain* (Edinburgh, 1709), Appendix, 22–31.

24. P. W. J. Riley, *The Union of England and Scotland: A Study in Anglo-Scottish Politics of the Eighteenth Century* (Manchester, 1978), 202, 214–9.

25. Ibid., 266–7.

26. Mitchison, *Lordship to Patronage*, 131–2.

27. C. A. Whatley, 'Economic Causes and Consequences of the Union of 1707: A Survey', *Scottish Historical Review*, LXVIII (1989), 158.

28. See, for example, Sir John Clerk's *History of the Union of Scotland and England* (Edinburgh, 1993), 133–4.

29. Macinnes, 'Studying the Scottish Estates and the Treaty of Union', *History Microcomputer Review*, 6, 2 (Fall 1990) 17.

30. See E. Richards, 'Scotland and the Uses of the Atlantic Empire', in B. Bailyn and P. D. Morgan (eds.), *Strangers Within the Realm: Cultural Margins of the First British Empire* (North Carolina, 1991), 71–6.

31. Whatley, 'Economic Causes', 156.

32. Smout, *Scottish Trade*, 253–9; J. Strawhorn, *The History of Ayr: Royal Burgh and County Town* (Edinburgh, 1989), 94.

33. T. M. Devine, 'The Union of 1707 and Scottish Development', *Scottish Economic & Social History*, 5 (1985), 25.

34. See Whatley, *Scottish Society*, 31–41.

35. E. J. Graham, 'In Defence of the Scottish Maritime Interest, 1681–1713', *Scottish Historical Review*, LXXI (1992), 88–104.

36. Whatley, *Scottish Society*, 39.

37. A. L. Murray, 'Administration and the Law', in T. I. Rae (ed.), *The Union of 1707: Its Impact on Scotland* (Glasgow, 1974), 34.

38. T. C. Smout, 'The Improvers and the Scottish Environment: Soils, Bogs and Woods', in Devine and Young, *Eighteenth Century Scotland*, 213–4.

39. I. Wallerstein, *The Modern World-System II: Mercantilism and the Consolidation of the European World-Economy, 1600–1750* (New York, 1980), 253.

40. Devine, 'The Union of 1707', 27.

41. Scott, *'The Boasted Advantages'*, 27.

42. Smout, 'The Burgh of Montrose', 183–4.

43. R. Mitchison, *A History of Scotland* (London, 1992 ed.), 311.

44. Clerk, *History of the Union*, 199–200.

45. Richards, 'Scotland and the Uses of the Atlantic Empire', 72.

46. J. Robertson, 'Andrew Fletcher's Vision of Union', in R. A. Mason (ed.), *Scotland and England, 1286–1815* (Edinburgh, 1987) 208.

47. Levack, *The Formation of the British State*, 160–6.

48. D. Szechi and D. Hayton, 'John Bull's Other Kingdoms: The English Government of Scotland and Ireland', in C. Jones (ed.), *Britain in the First Age of Party, 1680–1750* (London, 1987), 247.

49. Riley, *The Union of England and Scotland*, 165–6.

50. M. Hechter, *Internal Colonialism: The Celtic Fringe in British National Development, 1536–1966* (London, 1975), 71; on the War of the Spanish Succession and its consequences within the British Isles, see G. Holmes, *The Making of a Great Power: Late Stuart and Early Georgian Britain, 1660–1722* (London, 1993).

51. National Archives of Scotland, GD1/1158/4, Robert Harley to the Duke of Argyll, 17 July 1705.

52. See C. A. Whatley, *The Industrial Revolution in Scotland* (Cambridge, 1997), 9–17.

53. Whatley, 'Economic Causes', 159.

54. Riley, *The Union of England and Scotland*, 184.

55. J. M. Low, 'A Regional Example of the Mercantilist Theory of Economic Policy', *The Manchester School*, XXI (1953), 83.

56. Riley, *The Union of England and Scotland*, 42–3, 168.

57. Robertson, 'Andrew Fletcher's Vision', 209.

58. P. H. Scott, 'Bought and sold for English gold', *Chapman*, 69–70 (Autumn, 1992), 166.

59. G. H. Healey (ed.), *The Letters of Daniel Defoe* (Oxford, 1955), 156.

60. *Reports of the Royal Commission on Historical Manuscripts, Mar & Kellie Papers*, i (London, 1904) Earl of Mar to Sir David Nairne, 17 and 24 December 1706.

61. Riley, *The Union of England and Scotland*, 290.
62. Perth and Kinross Council Archives, Perth Burgh Records, B59/34/17/3, 'Stirling Address', 18 November 1706.
63. C. Kidd, 'Religious realignment between the Restoration and Union', in J. Roberstson (ed.), *A Union for Empire: Political Thought and the Union of 1707* (Cambridge, 1995), 165–7.
64. E. Henderson, *The Annals of Dunfermline, 1069–1878* (Dunfermline, 1878), 377–81.
65. Whatley, *Scottish Society*, 53; Healey, *Letters of Daniel Defoe*, 155–8.
66. *Reports of the Royal Commission on Historical Manuscripts, Mar and Kellie Papers*, i (London, 1904), Earl of Mar to Sir David Nairne, 31 December 1706.
67. Clerk, *History of the Union*, 150.
68. Smout, 'The Road to Union' in G. Holmes (ed.), *Britain after the Glorious Revolution* (London, 1969), 191.
69. MacKinnon, *The Union of England and Scotland*, 307–16.
70. Young, 'The Parliamentary Incorporating Union', 36–7.
71. See Whatley, 'How tame were the Scottish Lowlanders during the Eighteenth Century?' in T. M. Devine (ed.), *Conflict and Stability in Scottish Society, 1700–1850* (Edinburgh, 1990).
72. A. Lamont, 'Clubs against the Union of 1707', *Scottish Journal of Science*, I (1957), 219.
73. Macinnes, 'Studying the Scottish Estates', 16.
74. H. L. Snyder (ed.), The *Marlborough-Godolphin Correspondence (3 vols., Oxford, 1975)*, II, 727.
75. T. Harris, *London Crowds in the Reign of Charles II* (Cambridge, 1987), 35; N. Rogers, 'Popular Protest in Early Hanoverian London', *Past & Present*, 79 (1984).
76. See, for example, Whatley, *Scottish Society* (2000).

CHAPTER 4

Explaining the Union of 1707: An Interpretation

There was nothing inevitable about the parliamentary union which came into being in 1707. Although it had not always worked well, regal union held its own for much of the seventeenth century, and there are historians who rightly argue that it is mistaken to see it simply as a staging-post on the way to full union between Scotland and England. Even so, the tensions it created did place some sort of further union on the political agenda in the seventeenth century, both in theory, and has been seen, in (short-lived) practice. So it was not unexpected.

Nevertheless, experience elsewhere in Europe shows that whatever the final solution to Anglo-Scottish irritations, this did not necessarily have to take the form of an incorporating union. In Britain itself many other varieties of union – including economic and ecclesiastical – had been mooted in the preceding decades.

Yet early-modern monarchs, including the Stuarts and the Hanoverians, were anxious to strengthen their dynasties. Territorial expansion in order to pre-empt the emergence of usurpers was one means of achieving this. The international arena in the early-modern age was dangerous and unstable: security was often to be found in the nation-state. The geographical proximity of Scotland and England, and the fact that the people of both nations inhabited the same island, provided a certain logic of integration which was not always to be found in other European 'empires'; it was as an archipelagic composite state that Britain stood in contrast to the others, which were simply territorially contiguous. Union too could find a basis in a series of characteristics which the two countries had in greater or lesser degrees in common, such as their Protestantism, language, customs and political institutions. A growing volume of trade was conducted between them too, by sea and over the Border.

None of this explains why there was an incorporating union in 1707. Such considerations simply provide a background to it, as well as some justifications for political integration, several of which were advanced by early seventeenth-century unionists. These, it should be stressed, were usually Scotsmen. It was largely Scots who aspired to be British. It is a mistake, certainly at élite levels of society, to assume that anglicisation was equated with oppression: on the contrary, in the eyes of some contemporaries, closer contact with England was judged to be potentially politically liberating and economically advantageous. It was the periphery – Scotland – which was the 'benighted feudal province', not the metropolitan core. Even by the mid-eighteenth century, Britishness was still associated with Scottishness. It was Scots who were more anxious to 'complete' the Union, their 'Scotocentric patriotism' fuelled not by the fear of cultural repression but rather by the annoyance they felt that integration had only gone so far.[1]

There is a school of thought which argues that if there was a turning point, it was the instability of relations between England and Scotland which emerged after their respective 'revolutions' of 1688 and 1689. Paradoxically, the last, by sowing the seeds of increasingly bitter conflict between the two countries which were ruled by a single monarch, also led to the search for a new constitutional arrangement, that is something other than regal union. From the English point of view, this meant incorporating union.

Serious English interest in union was renewed in the early 1700s because of the actions taken by the newly assertive Scottish Parliament at a particular moment in English – and European – history. After 1694 Whigs and Tories vied at much more frequent elections for power at Westminster; Whigs looked to Scotland as a means of enhancing their numbers. The death of William in 1702 and the accession of Queen Anne (whose final surviving child, the Duke of Gloucester, had died in 1700) meant there was an even more pressing need to resolve the succession question in accordance with English requirements. These had been underlined in a postscript to the Treaty of the Hague (1702) which had committed England and its allies to fight on until France recognised the Protestant Succession in England. The War of the Spanish Succession roused English fears of the withdrawal of Scottish regiments, and, with the Cavalier party gaining ground in the election of 1703, perhaps of a Jacobite *coup* and subsequent push on her vulnerable northern frontier.

In 1706 Scotland probably had no choice but to accede to the broad thrust of England's proposals. The possibility that the English would resort to a military solution loomed in the background from the end of 1704, if not earlier, and concentrated minds. This, however, may have been bluster on England's part, and forgotten, along with union, with peace and the disappearance of the immediate crisis. There were precedents. Whatever the truth of this, there were those amongst the political élite in Scotland – the Earls of Cromarty, Mar, Seafield, Stair and Roxburghe, for example – who appear genuinely to have believed that an incorporating union would preserve 'the honour and liberties of Scotland' and the security of Britain. It should not be forgotten that by this time many of them were, after all, British politicians. The reality of the situation was that where it mattered, in relation to England, pre-Union Scotland was independent in name only. Court politicians in Scotland were as anxious to have troops on standby as Queen Anne and her English ministers were to send them. Their role would not have been to persuade the Scottish Parliament to approve the Articles, but to ensure that Parliament was not overthrown from outside.

Scotland's economic condition was critical, and much-discussed. A series of attempts on the part of the state to 'kick-start' the Scottish economy had produced nothing tangible, and there was a widespread recognition that in a mercantilist age Scotland was too weak on its own to conquer its problems of relative poverty and unemployment. Darien had made this brutally obvious, but even before this there had been a widespread recognition of Scottish under-achievement in comparison to other European economic entities. The Aliens Act threatened to make matters even worse. Patriotism came to be less concerned with national freedom than economic improvement.

Individual members of the Scottish Parliament, however, did have a choice. They could have voted against the Commissioners' proposals. Some did, on principle. The prospect of obtaining protected trading opportunities, however, persuaded a majority to opt for

union. Party discipline underpinned pro-Union votes. 'Political management', in all its forms, including bribery, both private and public,
was an integral part of the mechanism which kept adherents of the
Court party in line, and, critically, ensured the support of members of
the Squadrone Volante.

National and personal economic concerns, in various forms, were
at or near the top of the agenda. The former were served by the
guarantee that trade routes south would remain open, by the
protection of the Navigation Acts overseas, and by the monies to be
diverted from the Equivalent to the woollen industry. Scotsmen
however were not naive, and once it became clear that what was
being proposed was incorporating union, those with particular
economic interests who had any political clout sought determinedly
to ensure that these would be secured after 1707. There is a case for
maintaining that they were prepared to defy the Court – and
therefore endanger the entire union scheme – if they were ignored.
The form the Equivalent took was also the result of a clear-headed
recognition on the part of the Commissioners that they should
protect the interests of Scotland, both public and private. Clerk
dismissed the charge that the Commissioners had been unpatriotic –
traitors – in accepting the £398,085 payable as the Equivalent. On
the contrary, he argued, the Commissioners would have been 'trai-
torous and guilty' (or in the words of a modern historian, 'mad and
incompetent') had they not ensured that Scotland was to be compensated for taking on the burden of England's debts and
guaranteed the payment of arrears to those to whom they were
owed.[2]

Public opinion too played its part in determining the final form of
the Articles. In steering a way towards an agreement which would not
arouse English ire, but also make sufficient concessions to their
countrymen, Court politicians, Stair, Queensberry, and notably the
Earl of Mar, managed brilliantly. At the same time, however, it should
be acknowledged that the Union was carried by members of the
nation's political élite, against the wishes of the great majority.

The motives of those men who sought to feather their own nests
were not admirable but they are understandable. Together, however,
through the autumn of 1706, they fashioned a settlement which

would be to Scotland's advantage, or at least less to its disadvantage than might otherwise have been the case. Indeed some historians, particularly those with a nationalist bias, have failed to acknowledge the achievements of the stubborn and far from pliant Scots parliamentarians, who ensured the future of the Scottish church and several other major Scottish institutions such as the legal system and the rights and privileges of the Royal Burghs. As has been seen, this was jealously observed in Ireland.

The incorporating union of 1707 was neither inevitable nor a monument to wise and forward-looking statesmanship. And notwithstanding the claim that 'All contemporary accounts' say so,[3] nor was it a *diktat*. Scottish fears, about the independence of the Church of Scotland for example, were assuaged. The 'Explanations', too, secured concessions which simply would not have been granted had there not been an element of negotiation in the Treaty. That Scotland was permitted thereafter to operate as a 'semi-independent' political entity is further evidence that England's objective was not simply to impose its will on the Scots.

Nonetheless, there was a certain logic to it. It was an instance of early modern *realpolitik*, a practical agreement between unequal partners, born and made of political, economic and strategic necessity, which served the needs of the politicians of both countries at the time (although there were those who hoped that the Union would last). Viewed this way, that it has survived so long is truly remarkable. This, however, owes little to its creators and a lot more to those who worked it out. It has been a moveable feast, upheld on occasion, but more often ignored in the details. Whether the current constitutional mechanism will be sufficient to maintain it, since 1999 in its modified form, remains to be seen.

NOTES TO CHAPTER 4

1. C. Kidd, 'North Britishness and the nature of eighteenth-century British patriotisms', *Historical Journal*, 39 (1996) 365–7; C. Kidd, *Subverting Scotland's Past: Scottish Whig Historians and the Creation of an Anglo-British Identity, 1689–c.1830* (Cambridge, 1993), 205–6.

2. Sir John Clerk, *The History of the Union of Scotland and England* (Edinburgh, 1993), 151; J. S. Shaw, *The Political History of Eighteenth-Century Scotland* (Basingstoke, 1999), 13.

3. P. H. Scott, '*The Boasted Advantages*', 27.

Appendix 1.

Abbreviated version of William Seton of Pitmedden's
A Speech in Parliament On the First Article of the Treaty of Union (1706).

My Lord Chancellor

This Honourable House has heard the several *Articles of the Treaty of Union* twice read, has spent a considerable time in discoursing to each of them, and after much Debate is come to examine and determine upon the First: Notwithstanding all the Arguments offered against it, I cannot find the least Motive for altering the Opinion I had at Signing this Article, having had the Honour to be one of the Commissioners appointed by Her Majesty for that end; but that I may give all Satisfaction to every Member, I shall humbly offer in a plain manner my Thoughts in relation go it.

My Lord, this Article is the Foundation of the whole Treaty, and the Approving or Rejecting of it must determine Union or no Union betwixt both Kingdoms.

How far the Approving this Article conduces to our Happiness, appears evidently, by considering the three different Ways proposed for retriving the Languishing Condition of this Nation; which are; That we continue under the same Sovereign with *England* with Limitations on his Prerogative as King of *Scotland*; That the two Kingdoms be Incorporated into one, or that they be entirely separated.

That the Union of Crowns with Limitations on the Successor is not sufficient to rectifie the bad State of this Nation, appears from these Positions founded on Reason and Experience.

Two Kingdoms subject to one Sovereign, having different Interests, the nearer these are one to another, the greater Jealousie and Emulation will be betwixt 'em.

Every Monarch, having two or more Kingdoms, will be obliged to prefer the Counsel and Interest of the Stronger to that of the Weaker: and the greater Disparity of Power and Riches there is betwixt these

Kingdoms, the greater Influence, the more powerful Nation will have on the Sovereign. Notwithstanding these Positions, I shall suppose the Parliament of *Scotland* is vested with the Power of making Peace and War, of rewarding and punishing Persons of all Ranks, of Levying Troops, and of the *Negative* itself.

I cou'd show the Inconveniences, that must attend such a State of Government in Disposal of Places and managing Publick Affairs; I cou'd likewise show the Improbability of attaining such Conditions, or keeping 'em if attained; but laying aside such Considerations, my humble Opinion is, That we cannot reap any Benefit from these Conditions of Government, without the Assistance of *England*: and the People thereof will never be convinced to promote the Interest of *Scotland*, 'till both Kingdoms are Incorporated into One: So that I conceive such a State of Limitations to be no better for *Scotland*, than if it were intirely separated from *England*, in which State there's little Appearance of procuring any Remedy to our present Circumstances, which appears from these uncontraverted Positions.

The People and Government of *Scotland* must be Richer or Poorer, as they have Plenty or Scarcity of Money, the common Measure of Trade.

No Money or Things of Value can be purchased in the Course of Commerce: but where there's a Force to protect it.

This Nation is behind all other Nations of *Europe* for many years, with respect to the Effects of an extended Trade.

This Nation being Poor and without Force to protect it's Commerce, cannot reap great Advantages by it, till it partake of the Trade and Protection of some powerful Neighbour Nation, that can communicate both these . . .

My Lord, I'm sorry, that in place of Things we amuse ourselves with Words; for my part I comprehend no durable Union betwixt *Scotland* and *England*, but that expressed in this Article by *One Kingdom*, that is to say, One People, One Civil Government and One Interest.

'Tis true, the Words, *Federal Union*, are become very Fashionable, and may be handsomely fitted to delude unthinking People; But if any Member of this House will give himself the Trouble, to examine what Conditions or Articles are understood by these Words, and reduce them into any kind of Federal Compacts, whereby distinct

Nations have been United: I'll presume to say, These will be found
Impracticable, or of very little Use to us.

But to put that Matter in a clear Light, these *Queries* ought to be
duly examined, Whether a Federal Union be Practicable betwixt two
Nations accustomed to a Monarchical Government? Whether there
can be any sure Guaranty projected for the Observance of the
Articles of a Federal Compact, stipulated betwixt two Nations;
whereof the one is much Superior to the other in Riches, Numbers of
People, and an extended Commerce? Whether the Advantages of a
Federal Union do Ballance its Disadvantages? Whether the *English*
will accept a Federal Union, supposing it to be for the true Interest of
both Nations? Whether any Federal Compact betwixt *Scotland* and
England, is sufficient to secure the Peace of this Island, or Fortify it
against the Intrigues and Invasions of its Foreign Enemies? And
whether *England* in Prudence, ought to Communicate its Trade and
Protection to this Nation, till both Kingdoms are incorporated into
one? . . .

I cou'd give some Account of the particular Advantages we'll
obtain by an Incorporating Union with *England*, but there will be
occasions to Discourse of these, as the other Articles fall under the
Consideration of this Parliament. In general, I may assert, That by
this Union, we'll have Access to all the Advantages in Commerce,
the *English* enjoy; we'll be capable, by a good Government, to
Improve our National Product, for the benefit of the whole Island;
and we'll have our Liberty, Property and Religion, secured under the
Protection of one Sovereign, and one Parliament of *Great Britain*.

Now, *My Lord*, If Limitations on the Successor can be of little or no
Use to us; if an entire Separation from *England* brings no Advantage
to this Nation: and if all Federal Compacts, as we are stated, have
insuperable Difficulties, which in some measure I have cleared,
there's but one of two left to our Choise, *to wit*, That both Kingdoms
be united into one, or that we continue under the same Sovereign
with *England* as we have done these 100 years past. This last I
conceive to be a very ill State, for by it (if Experience be convincing)
we cannot expect any of the Advantages of an Incorporating Union;
but on the contrair, Our Sovereignty and Independency will be
eclipsed, the number of our Nobility will Encrease, Our Commons

will be Oppressed, Our Parliaments will be influenced by *England*, the Execution of our Laws will be neglected; Our Peace will be interrupted by Factions for Places and Pensions; Luxury together with Poverty (tho' strange) will invade us; Numbers of *Scots* will withdraw themselves to Foreign Countries; and all the other Effects of Bad Government must necessarily attend us.

Let us therefore, *My Lord*, after all these Considerations approve this Article: and when the whole Treaty shall be duly examined and ratified, I'm hopeful, this Parliament will return their most Dutiful Acknowledgments to Her Majesty, for Her Royal Endeavours in promoting a Lasting Union betwixt both Nations.

Appendix 2.

Letter from the Duke of Argyll to the Earl of Mar, 18 July 1706 (*Reports of the Royal Commission on Historical Manuscripts, 60, Mar and Kellie Papers*, i, London, 1904, p. 270).

1706, July 18. Camp at St. Luis le Tere. – I should have receiv'd your letter before Ostend, but so it is I had it only this morning. I am extremely sorry that all my friends should desire me to doe what for aught I can as yet see I shall not be able to comply with. My Lord, it is surprising to me that my Lord Treasurer, who is a man of sense, should think of sending me up and down like a footman from one country to another without ever offering me any reward. Thier is indeed a sairtin service due from every subject to his Prince, and that I shall pay the Queen as fathfully as any body can doe; but if her ministers thinks it for her service to imploy me any forder I doo think the proposall should be attended with an offer of a reward. But I am so fare from beeing treated in this manner that I cannot obtain justice even in the army, where I doe flatter my selfe I have dun the Queen as much service, to say no more, as anybody in my station. My Lord, when I have justice dun me here and am told what to expect for going to Scotland, I shall be reddy to obey my Lord Treasurer's commands. Till then I hope my friends will think it fitt I stay here, unless I have sum body put over my head; and in that cais I shall lett my Lord Marlboro give my post to sumbody who chances to be more to his mind, which will be a very noble reward for my service and I'll goe and hear Camilla in her own country.

Appendix 3.

Letter from John Philp to William Lorimer, the Earl of Seafield's chamberlain at Cullen, 6 February 1707 (J Grant, ed., *Seafield Correspondence, 1685–1708,* Edinburgh, 1912, pp. 429–30).

Edinburgh, febry. 6, 1707

I wrote formerly to you about the purchase of yor uncles houses. Am satisfied with the disposition, if it contains the warrandice, but by Mrs. Lorimers letter she seems to scruple it. You'll need to advyse her, and if she pleases I'll pay her interest for her money till Whytsunday next, though it will be above a years at rent loss upon any money that people may have in there hands att that, if the union succeed, for no species y^r after will pass, but att the English rates of fyve shillings the crown, and so proportionally. The Parliat. inclynes to make up the loss of the money out of the equivalent, but that's uncertain and will take a time to be good. For guineas they'll pass att no more than 21^s and 6^d ster. and no reparation for the loss. I send you accompt of the proceedings of Parlia^t by these minutes. They'll best inform you. Scotland is exempted from the malt tax dureing the warr, and in time of peace its never imposed. For what all the nobility and gentry brews they are to pay no excyse. Ale sold above two shilling the pint payes 4^s and 9^d sterline of excyse for 10 gallons. This will very little affect the north. When my Lords wictuall comes up send me two bolls of best meal and I'll pay you. Perhaps William Strachan may give it in pairt of his rent for the lands he has in Bruntowne. If he doe, let it be good, and if wee be gone to London advyse Mr. Stewart or Will. Gardne to send it to my wife ... I am, D.C., Your most affectionat cousine and servant,

JOHN PHILP.

Appendix 4.

Extract from letter from the Earl of Mar to Sir David Nairne, 7 December 1706

(Reports of the Royal Commission on Historical Manuscripts, 60, Mar and Kellie Papers, i, London, 1904, pp. 348–9).

1706, December 7. Edinburgh. – In my letter to my Lord Halifax, I said that I hopt any alteratione or additione as to the malt might be gott done here by way of address to her Majestie; but by what was done that day you see I was mistaken. For with a great strugle and by the Chancellor's casting vote wee carried onlie that the exemptione should be dureing this war, and not a certaine number of years, which wou'd have been seven at least, and very probabilie thertein or ninetein if we had lost the vote. The addressing the Queen upon it was proposed, but wee cou'd not get it to take in the House. Yesterday wee were on the 14th artickle again, and the opposers proposed that an exemption for Scotland as to all taxes whatsomever should be aded, except such as are alreadie agreed to. Some proposed this for a certain number of years, and others dureing the war. This batle was strongly fought, and we toke a vast deall of paines to gaine people to approve of the artickle as it was, now since that concerning the malt was added for which they were so affraid. It is needless to tell you all that was said in the House upon this; but some of us spoke a great dale and with all the earnestness we cou'd, and the opposers were not silent, I can assure you. They used all the populare and plausable arguments they cou'd feind, and by them deluded severall people. However, wee at last brought it to a questione. Wee were forced to have a previous vote what shou'd be the state of the question, which wee carried by 18; then the artickle was approven by 38. The necessity that was of yealding to explanationes or alterations plainly appears by Thursday's procedor; but now since wee carried the artickle without any other alteratione I hope that of the malt will not be thought inconsistent with the Treatie, so will be no stope to its passing in England. Scotland by the

Treatie was not only to by free of the present malt tax, but also of any
that shou'd by imposed upon England this Session of the Parliament
there. This tax is never imposed but in tim of war, and I hope this war
will be at an end before the ensewing campaigne be over. For my self
I did wish with others that there had been no addition to or exception
from this 14th artickle, for I thought Scotland very saife with the
reference to the Parliament of Britain, who will certainlie be tender of
us in the infancie of the Union, when we are poor, and it will take
some years to make us feel the advantadges of the communication of
trade; so shou'd greater taxes be imposed upon us imediatlie after the
Union than Scotland boar before it, and before the generality of this
kingdom found the sueet and advantages of being incorporat, it
wou'd certainlie have bad effects and be very griveous to the people.
This will certainlie be under the consideration of the Parliament of
Britain, so without any express stipulation I wou'd have thought
Scotland shure of being free of any malt tax this war, and I did all in
my power to persuade others to be of the sam oppinion; but ther is
such an apprehension here of the griveousness of this tax that wee
cou'd not gett a plurality by a great odds to be against the additione,
tho' wee gott them to trust to the Parliament of Britain for being free
of any other imposition. And since it is so, I hope the addition will
give no umbradge nor offence to our neighbours. Pray give my
humble service to my Lord Halyfax and show him this, because I was
mistaken in mine to his Lordship as to what wou'd be done upon this
point. The artickle about the salt is commited you know. I confess
I'm more affraid of that than any artickle now remaining, but I hope
if any alteration be inevitable wee shall carrie it so as not [to be]
inconsistent with the Treatie; which is all I can say as to that untill
wee gett a report from the comittie and see what turn it is like to take
in the House . . .

Appendix 5.

Petition, Stirling Town Council against the proposed
incorporating union, 18 November 1706
(Perth and Kinross Council Archives,
Perth Burgh Archives, B 59/34/17/3).

To His Grace Her Majesties high Commissioner and the Estates of
Parliament. The Address of the provost Baillies Town Councill and
other Inhabitants of the Burgh of Stirling.

Humbly Sheweth

That having had our most deliberat thoughts upon the great affair
of the Union of the two Nationes, as Contained in the printed Articles,
wee judge it our Indispensable duety to the Nation to this place, yea to
posterity, with all Imaginable defference to your Grace and Honourable Estates of parliament humbly to represent, That though we are
desirous that true pecae and friendship be perpetually Cultivat with
our neighbours in England, Upon on Just and honourable termes
consisting with the being, Soveraigntie & Independence of our
Natione and parliaments as defenders therof, Yet we judge your
goeing into this Treaty as it now Lyes before you, will bring ane
Insupportable burden of Taxationes upon this Land, which all the
Grants of freedome of Trade will never Counterballance being so
uncertain and precariuous while still under the regulationes of the
English in the parliament of Brittain, who may if they please discour-
age the most Considerable Branches of our Trade, if any way
apprehended to interfeir with their own. That it will prove, ruining to
our manufactores, That it will ane exposing of our Religione, Church
Government as by Law Established, our Claime of Right, Lawes,
Liberties & Consequently all that's valuable, To be incroached upon,
yea wholly Subverted by them, whose principles does, & Suposed
Interests may Lead yr Unto, That it will be a depryving of us and the
rest of the royall burghs in this Natione, in a great measure of our
fundamentall right and propertie of being represented in the Legis
Lative power, That therby one of the most ancient nationes so long

and gloriously defended by our worthie patriots will be supprest. Our parliaments the very hedge of all that is dear to us, Extinguished and we and our posterity brought under ane Lasting yoke which we will never be able to bear, The fatall consequences of which we tremble to think upon.

We therefore conforme to the privielege allowed to us in our Claim of right, most humbly Supplicat and firmly expect from your Grace and the Honourable Estates of parliament That ye will not conclude ane Incorporating Union Soe Destructive to many and Dangerous to the whole of these things which are dear to us, That ye will be pleased to Lay the evident Danger therof before Our Most Gracious Queen that some reliefs may be Granted untill some expedient be found out for the more universall Satisfactione of her majesties Good Subjects, That ye will so Setle the State of this Nation as the hopes and attempts of all popish pretenders Whatsomever may be forever defeat, That ye will maintain and support the true reformed protestant Religion the Government of this Nationall Church as now by Law established, The Sovereignty & Independency of this Natione in all its Liberties Sacred and Civill the undoubted properties of every Member of this Realme That ye will maintaine and defend the Rights and Being of our parliaments & our privilege of Still being represented therein without which we Cannot reckon our Selves secure in the possession of those things soe valuable in themselves, and which we are resolved to defend with our Lives and fortunes According to our Laws and claime of right. Subscrybed be us at Stirling the eighteenth day of November 1706.

Appendix 6.

The Articles of the Treaty of Union of 1707, with the amendments* inserted by the Scottish Estates during the 'Explanations'

The Articles of Union are rarely published and read in full, and therefore only partial impressions of their range are given. The 'explanations' were a series of amendments to the Articles of Union which were added by the Scottish Parliament during the late autumn of 1706. Historians disagree about their significance, and also, of course, about the role of economic considerations in general in the 'making' of the Act of Union.

I   That the two Kingdoms of Scotland and England, shall, upon the first Day of May next ensuing the Date hereof, and for ever after, be united into one Kingdom by the Name of Great-Britain, and that the Ensigns Armorial of the said united Kingdom, be such as her Majesty shall appoint; and the Crosses of St. *Andrew* and St. *George* be conjoined in such a manner as her Majesty shall think fit, and used in all Flags, Banners, Standards, and Ensigns, both at Sea and Land.

II   That the Succession to the Monarchy of the united Kingdom of Great-Britain, and of the Dominions thereunto belonging, after her most sacred Majesty, and in default of Issue of her Majesty, be, remain, and continue to the most Excellent Princess Sophia, Electress and Duchess Dowager of Hanover, and the Heirs of her Body, being Protestants, upon whom the Crown of England is settled, by an Act of Parliament made in England, in the twelfth Year of the Reign of his late Majesty King William the Third, entitled, *An Act for further Limitation of the Crown, and better securing the Rights and Liberties of the Subject.* And that all Papists, and Persons marrying Papists, shall be excluded from, and for ever incapable to inherit, possess, or enjoy the imperial Crown of Great-Britain, and the Dominions thereunto belonging, or any Part thereof. And in every such Case, the Crown

* The amendments are italicised.

and Government shall from Time to Time descend to, and be enjoyed by such Person, being a Protestant, as should have inherited and enjoyed the same, in case such Papist, or Person marrying a Papist, was naturally dead, according to the Provision for the Descent of the Crown of England, made by another Act of Parliament in England, in the first Year of the Reign of their late Majesties King William and Queen Mary, entitled, *An Act declaring the Rights and Liberties of the Subject, and settling the Succession of the Crown.*

III   That the united Kingdom of Great-Britain be represented by one and the same Parliament, to be stiled the Parliament of Great-Britain.

IV   That all the Subjects of the united Kingdom of Great-Britain shall, from and after the Union, have full Freedom and Intercourse of Trade and Navigation, to and from any Port or Place within the said united Kingdom, and the Dominions and Plantations thereunto belonging; and that there be a Communication of all other Rights, Privileges, and Advantages, which do or may belong to the Subjects of either Kingdom, except where it is otherwise expressly agreed in these Articles.

V   That all Ships or Vessels, belonging to her Majesty's Subjects of Scotland, at the Time of *ratifying the Treaty of Union of the two Kingdoms, in the Parliament of Scotland,* though foreign built, be deemed, and pass as Ships of the Build of Great-Britain; the Owner, or where there are more Owners, one or more of the Owners, within twelve Months after the first of May next, making Oath, that, at the Time of *ratifying the Treaty of Union in the Parliament of Scotland,* the same did, *in whole, or in part,* belong to him or them, or to some other Subject or Subjects of Scotland, to be particularly named, with the Place of their respective Abodes; and that the same doth then, *at the time of the said Deposition,* wholly belong to him, or them, and that no Foreigner, directly or indirectly, hath any Share, Part, or Interest therein, Which Oath shall be made before the chief Officer or Officers of the Customs, in the Port next to the Abode of the said Owner or Owners: And the said Officer or Officers, shall be empowered to administrate the said Oath: And the Oath being so administrated, shall be attested by the Officer or Officers, who administrated the same. And, being registered by the said Officer or Officers, shall be delivered to the Master of the Ship for Security of her Navigation; and a Duplicate thereof shall be transmitted by the said Officer or Officers, to the chief Officer or Officers of the Customs in the Port of Edinburgh, to be there entered in a Register, and from thence to be sent to the Port of London, to be there entered in the general Register of all trading Ships belonging to Great-Britain.

VI   That all Parts of the united Kingdom, for ever, from and after the Union, shall have the same Allowances, Encouragements, and Draw-backs, and be under the same Prohibitions, Restrictions, and Regulations of Trade, and liable to the same Customs and Duties, and Import and Export. And that the Allowances, Encouragements, *and draw-backs*, Prohibitions, Restrictions, and Regulations, of Trade, and the Customs and Duties on Import and Export settled in England, when the Union commences, shall, from and after the Union, take place throughout the whole united Kingdom: *Excepting and reserving the Duties upon Export and Import, of such particular Commodities, from which any Persons, the Subjects of either Kingdom, are specially liberated and exempted by their private Rights, which, after the Union, are to remain safe and entire to them in all respects, as before the same. And that from, and after the Union, no Scots Cattle carried into England, shall be liable to any other Duties, either on the public or private Accounts, than these Duties, to which the Cattle of England are, or shall be liable within the said Kingdom. And seeing, by the Laws of England, there are Rewards granted upon the Exportation of certain kinds of Grain, wherein Oats grinded or ungrinded are not expressed, that from, and after the Union, when Oats shall be sold at fifteen Shillings Sterling per Quarter, or under, there shall be paid two Shillings and Six-pence Sterling for every Quarter of the Oatmeal exported, in the Terms of the Law, whereby, and so long as Rewards are granted for Exportation of other Grains; and that the Beer of Scotland, have the same Reward as Barley: And in respect the Exportation of Victual into Scotland from any Place beyond Sea, would prove a Discouragement to Tillage, therefore that the Prohibition, as now in Force by the Law of Scotland, against Importation of Victual from Ireland, or any other Place beyond Sea into Scotland, do, after the Union, remain in the same Force as now it is, until more proper and effectual Ways be provided by the Parliament of Great-Britain, for discouraging the Importation of the said Victual from beyond Sea.*

VII   That all Parts of the united Kingdom be for ever, from, and after the Union, liable to the same Excises upon all excisable Liquors,

Excepting only that the thirty four Gallons English Barrel of Beer or Ale, amounting to twelve Gallons Scots present Measure, sold in Scotland by the Brewer at nine Shillings Six pence Sterling, excluding all Duties, and retailed, including Duties, and the Retailers Profit at two Pence the Scots Pint, or eighth Part of the Scots Gallon, be not after the Union liable on account of the present Excise upon excisable Liquors in England; to any higher Imposition than two Shillings Sterling upon the foresaid thirty-four Gallons English Barrel, being twelve Gallons the present Scots Measure. 'And that the Excise settled in England on *all other Liquors,* when the Union commences, take place throughout the whole united Kingdom.

VIII   That, from and after the Union, all foreign Salt which shall be imported into Scotland, shall be charged at the Importation there, with the same Duties as the like Salt is now charged with being imported into England, and to be levied and secured in the same manner. *But in regard the Duties of great Quantities of foreign Salt imported, may be very heavy upon the Merchants Importers, that therefore all foreign Salt imported into Scotland, shall be cellered and locked up under the Custody of the Merchant Importer, and the Officers employed for levying the Duties upon Salt; and that the Merchant may have what Quantities thereof his Occasions may require, not under a Weigh or forty Bushels at a Time, giving Security for the Duty, of what Quantities he receives, payable in six Months.* But Scotland shall, for the space of seven Years, from the said Union, be exempted from paying in Scotland for Salt made there, the Duty or Excise now payable for Salt made in England: but, from the Expiration of the said seven Years, shall be subject and liable to the same Duties as Salt made in England, to be levied and secured in the same manner, and with proportionable Draw-backs and Allowances as in England, with this Exception, *That Scotland shall, after the said seven Years, remain exempted from the Duty of two Shillings and four Pence the Bushel on home-Salt, imposed by an Act made in England in the ninth and tenth Years of King William the Third of England; and if the Parliament of Great-Britain shall, at, or before the expiring of the said seven Years, substitute any other Fund, in place of the said two Shillings and four Pence of Excise upon the Bushel of home Salt, Scotland shall, after the said seven Years, bear a Proportion of the said Fund, and have an Equivalent in the Terms of this Treaty.* And that, during the said seven Years, there shall be paid in England for all Salt made in Scotland, and imported from thence into England, the same Duties upon the Importation, as shall be payable for Salt made in England, to be levied and secured in the same manner as the Duties on foreign Salt are to be levied and secured in England. And that, after the said seven Years, *how long the said Duty of two Shillings four Pence a Bushel upon Salt is continued in England, the said two Shillings four Pence a Bushel, shall be payable for all Salt made in Scotland, and imported into England, to be levied and secured in the same manner; and that during the Continuance of the Duty of two Shillings four Pence a Bushel upon Salt made in England,* no Salt whatsoever be brought from Scotland to England by Land in any manner, under the Penalty of forfeiting the Salt, and the Cattle and Carriages made use of in bringing the same, and paying twenty Shillings for every Bushel of such Salt, and proportionably for a greater or lesser Quantity, for which the Carrier as well as the Owner shall be liable, jointly and severally, and the Persons bringing or carrying the same, to be imprisoned by any one Justice of the Peace, by the space of six Months without Bail, and until the Penalty be paid. And, for establishing an Equality in Trade, that all Flesh exported from Scotland to England, and put on Board in Scotland, to be exported to Ports beyond the Sea, *and Provisions for Ships in Scotland, and for foreign Voyages, may be salted with Scots Salt, paying the same Duty for what Salt is so employed, as the like Quantity of such Salt pays in England and under the same Penalties, Forfeitures and Provisions, for preventing of such Frauds as are mentioned in the Laws of England:* And that, from and after the Union, the Laws and Acts of Parliament in Scotland for pineing, curing and packing of Herrings, white Fish and Salmon, for Exportation with foreign Salt only, *without any Mixture of British or Irish Salt;* and for preventing of Frauds, in curing and packing of Fish, be continued in Force in Scotland, subject to such Alterations as shall be made by the Parliament of Great-Britain; and that all Fish exported from Scotland to Parts beyond the Seas, which shall be cured with foreign Salt only, *and without Mixture of British or Irish Salt, shall have the same Eases, Premiums and Draw-backs, as are or shall be allowed to such Persons as export the like Fish from England:* And that for Encouragement of the Herring-fishing, *there shall be allowed and payed to the Subjects, Inhabitants of Great-Britain, during the present Allowances for other Fishes, ten Shillings five Pence Sterling for every Barrel of white Herring, which shall be exported from Scotland; and that they shall be allowed five Shillings Sterling for every Barrel of Beef or Pork salted with foreign Salt, without Mixture of British or Irish Salt, and exported for Sale from Scotland to Parts beyond Sea, alterable by the Parliament of Great-Britain.* And if any Matters of Frauds, relating to the said Duties on Salt, shall hereafter appear, which are not sufficiently provided against by this Article, the same shall be subject to such further Provisions, as shall be thought fit by the Parliament of Great-Britain.

IX   That whenever the Sum of one Million nine hundred ninety-seven Thousand, seven Hundred and sixty-three Pounds, eight Shillings, four Pence Half-penny, shall be enacted by the Parliament of Great-Britain, to be raised in that Part of the united Kingdom, now called England, on Land and other Things usually charged in Acts of Parliament there, for granting an Aid to the Crown by a Land-Tax; that Part of the united Kingdom, now called Scotland, shall be charged by the same Act, with a further Sum of forty-eight thousand Pounds, free of all Charges, as the Quota of Scotland to such Tax, and so proportionably for any greater or lesser Sum raised in England, by any Tax on Land, and other Things usually charged, together with the Land; and that such Quota for Scotland, in the Cases aforesaid, be raised and collected in the same manner as the Cess now is in Scotland, but subject to such Regulations in the manner of collecting, as shall be made by the Parliament of Great-Britain.

X   That, during the continuance of the respective Duties on stamped Paper, Vellum and Parchment, by the several Acts now in Force in England, Scotland shall not be charged with the same respective Duties.

XI   That, during the continuance of the Duties payable in England on Windows and Lights, which determines on the first Day of August, one thousand seven hundred and ten, Scotland shall not be charged with the same Duties.

XII   That, during the continuance of the Duties payable in England on Coals, Culm and Cinders, which determines the thirtieth Day of September, one thousand seven hundred and ten, Scotland shall not be charged therewith for Coals, Culm and Cinders consumed there, but shall be charged with the same Duties as in England, for all Coals, Culm and Cinders not consumed in Scotland.

XIII   That, during the continuance of the Duty payable in England on Malt, which determines the twenty-fourth Day of June, one thousand seven hundred and seven, Scotland shall not be charged with that Duty.

XIV   That the Kingdom of Scotland be not charged with any other Duties, laid on by the Parliament of England before the Union, except those consented to in this Treaty; in regard it is agreed, that all necessary Provision shall be made by the Parliament of Scotland, for the public Charge and Service of that Kingdom, for the Year one thousand seven hundred and seven; providing nevertheless, that, if the Parliament of England shall think fit to lay any further Impositions, by way of Custom, or such Excises, with which, by Virtue of this Treaty, Scotland is to be charged equally with England; in such Case, Scotland shall be liable to the same Customs and Excises, and have an Equivalent to be settled, by the Parliament of Great-Britain, with this further Provision, *That any Malt to be made and consumed in that Part of the united Kingdom now called Scotland, shall not be charged with any Imposition on Malt during this War.* And seeing it cannot be supposed, that the Parliament of Great-Britain will ever lay any sort of Burthens upon the united Kingdom, but what they shall find of necessity, at that Time, for the Preservation and Good of the whole; and with due Regard to the Circumstances and Abilities of every Part of the united Kingdom; therefore, it is agreed, that there be no further Exemption insisted on for any Part of the united Kingdom, but that the Consideration of any Exemptions beyond what is already agreed on in this Treaty, shall be left to the Determination of the Parliament of Great Britain.

XV   That whereas by the Terms of this Treaty, the Subjects of Scotland, for preserving an Equality of Trade throughout the united Kingdom, will be liable to several Customs and Excises now payable in England, which will be applicable towards payment of the Debts of England, contracted before the Union; it is agreed, That Scotland shall have an Equivalent for what the Subjects thereof shall be so charged, towards Payment of the said Debts of England, in all Particulars whatsoever, in manner following, *viz.* That, before the Union of the said Kingdoms, the Sum of three hundred ninety-eight Thousand, and eighty-five Pounds ten Shillings, be granted to her Majesty by the Parliament of England, for the Uses after mentioned, being the Equivalent, to be answered to Scotland, for such Parts of the said Customs, and Excises upon all excisable Liquors, with which that Kingdom is to be charged upon the Union, as will be applicable to the Payment of the said Debts of England, according to the Proportions which the present Customs in Scotland, being thirty thousand Pounds *per Annum*, do bear to the Customs in England, computed at one Million, three hundred forty-one Thousand, five hundred and fifty-nine Pounds *per Annum*: And which the present Excises on excisable Liquors in Scotland, being thirty-three thousand and five hundred Pounds *per Annum*, do bear to the Excises on excisable Liquors in England, computed at nine hundred forty-seven Thousand, six hundred and two Pounds *per Annum;* which Sum of three hundred ninety-eight Thousand, eighty-five Pounds ten Shillings, shall be due and payable from the Time of the Union: And in regard, that, after the Union, Scotland becoming liable to the same Customs and Duties payable on Import and Export, and to the same Excises on all excisable Liquors, as in England, as well upon that Account, as upon the Account of the Increase of Trade and People, (which will be the happy Consequence of the Union) the said Revenues will much improve beyond the before-mentioned annual Values thereof, of which no present Estimate can be made; yet, nevertheless, for the Reasons aforesaid, there ought to be a reasonable Equivalent answered to Scotland; it is agreed, That, after the Union, there shall be an Account kept of the said Duties arising in Scotland, to the end it may appear, what ought to be answered to Scotland, as an Equivalent for such Proportion of the said Increase, as shall be applicable to the Payment of the Debts of England. And for the further, and more effectual answering the several Ends hereafter mentioned, it is agreed, That, from and after the Union, the whole Increase of the Revenues of Customs, and Duties on Import and Export, and Excises upon excisable Liquors in Scotland, over and above the annual Produce of the said respective Duties, as above stated, shall go, and be applied, for the Term of seven Years, to the Uses hereafter mentioned, and that, upon the said Account, there shall be answered to Scotland, annually, from the end of seven Years after the Union, an Equivalent in Proportion to such Part of the said Increase, as shall be applicable to the Debts of England: *And generally, that an Equivalent shall be answered to Scotland, for such Parts of the English*

Debts as Scotland may hereafter become liable to pay, by reason of the Union, other than such for which Appropriations have been made by Parliament in England, of the Customs or other Duties on Export and Import, Excises on all exciseable Liquors, in respect of which Debts, Equivalents are herein before provided. And as for the Uses to which the said Sum of three hundred ninety-eight Thousand, eighty-five Pounds ten Shillings, to be granted as aforesaid, and all other Monies which are to be answered or allowed to Scotland, as said is, are to be applied, it is agreed, *That, in the first place, out of the foresaid Sum,* what Consideration shall be found necessary to be had for any Losses which private Persons may sustain, by reducing the Coin of Scotland, to the Standard and Value of the Coin of England, may be made good. In the next place, that the capital Stock, or Fund of the African and Indian Company of Scotland, advanced together with the Interest for the said capital Stock, after the Rate of *5 per Cent. per Annum,* from the respective Times of the Payment thereof, shall be paid; upon Payment of which capital Stock and Interest, it is agreed, The said Company be dissolved and cease; and also, that, from the Time of passing the Act of Parliament in England, for raising the said Sum of three hundred ninety-eight Thousand, eighty-five Pounds ten Shillings, the said Company shall neither trade, nor grant Licence to trade, providing, *That if the said Stock and Interest shall not be paid in twelve Months after the Commencement of the Union, that then the said Company may from thence forward trade, or give Licence to trade, until the said whole capital Stock and Interest shall be paid.* And as to the Overplus of the said Sum of three hundred ninety-eight Thousand, eighty-five Pounds ten Shillings, after Payment of what Consideration shall be had for Losses, in repairing the Coin, and paying the said capital Stock and Interest; and also the whole Increase of the said Revenues of Customs, Duties, and Excises, above the present Value, which shall arise in Scotland, during the said Term of seven Years, together with the Equivalent which shall become due, upon the Improvement thereof in Scotland after the said Term *of seven Years*: and also, as to all other Sums, which, according to the Agreements aforesaid, may become payable to Scotland, by way of Equivalent, for what that Kingdom shall hereafter become liable, towards Payment of the Debts of England: it is agreed, That the same may be applied in the manner following, *viz. That all the public Debts of the Kingdom of Scotland, as shall be adjusted by the present Parliament, shall be paid: And that two thousand Pounds per annum for the space of seven Years, shall be applied towards encouraging and promoting the Manufacture of coarse Wool, within those Shires which produce the Wool; and that the first two thousands Sterling be paid at Martinmas next, and so yearly at Martinmas during the Space aforesaid.* And afterwards the same shall be wholly applied towards the encouraging and promoting the Fisheries, and such other Manufactories and Improvements in Scotland, as may most conduce to the general good of the united Kingdom. And it is agreed, That her Majesty be empowered to appoint Commissioners, who shall be accountable to the Parliament of Great-Britain, for disposing the said Sum of three hundred ninety-eight thousand and eighty-five Pounds, ten Shillings; and all other Monies which shall arise to Scotland, upon the Agreements aforesaid, to the Purposes before mentioned: Which Commissioners shall be empowered to call for, receive, and dispose of the said Monies in Manner aforesaid; and to inspect the Books of the several Collectors of the said Revenues, and of all other Duties, from whence an Equivalent may arise, and that the Collectors and Managers of the said Revenues and Duties, be obliged to give to the said Commissioners, subscribed, authentic Abbreviates of the Produce of such Revenues and Duties arising in their respective Districts: And that the said Commissioners shall have their Office within the Limits of Scotland, and shall in such Office keep Books, containing Accounts of the Amount of the Equivalents, and how the same shall have been disposed of from time to time; which may be inspected by any of the Subjects who shall desire the same.

XVI   That, from and after the Union, the Coin shall be of the same Standard and Value throughout the united Kingdom, as now in England, and a Mint shall be continued in Scotland, under the same Rules as the Mint in England, *and the present Officers of the Mint continued*, subject to such Regulations and Alterations as her Majesty, her Heirs or Successors, or the Parliament of Great-Britain, shall think fit.

XVII   That, from and after the Union, the same Weights and Measures shall be used throughout the united Kingdom, as are now established in England: and Standards of Weights and Measures shall be kept by those Burghs in Scotland, to whom the keeping the

Standards of Weights and Measures, now in use there, does of special Right belong. All which Standards shall be sent down to such respective Burghs, from the Standards kept in the Exchequer at Westminster, subject nevertheless to such Regulations as the Parliament of Great-Britain shall think fit.

XVIII   That the Laws concerning Regulation of Trade, Customs, and such Excises, to which Scotland is, by virtue of this Treaty, to be liable, be the same in Scotland, from and after the Union, as in England; and that all other laws in use, within the Kingdom of *Scotland*, do, after the Union, and notwithstanding thereof, remain in the same Force as before, (except such as are contrary to, or inconsistent with this Treaty) but alterable by the Parliament of Great-Britain, with this Difference betwixt the Laws concerning public Right, Polity, and Civil Government, and those which concern private Right: that the Laws which concern public Right, Polity and Civil Government, may be made the same throughout the whole united Kingdom; but that no Alteration be made in Laws which concern private Right, except for evident Utility of the Subjects within Scotland.

XIX   That the Court of Session, or College of Justice, do, after the Union, and notwithstanding thereof, remain, in all time coming, within Scotland, as it is now constituted by the Laws of that Kingdom, and with the same Authority and Privileges, as before the Union, subject nevertheless to such Regulations for the better Administration of Justice, as shall be made by the Parliament of Great Britain; *And that hereafter none shall be named by her Majesty and her Royal Successors, to be ordinary Lords of Session, but such who have served in the College of Justice as Advocates, or principal Clerks of Session for the Space of five Years; or as Writers to the Signet, for the Space of ten Years: with this Provision, that no Writer to the Signet be capable to be admitted a Lord of the Session, unless he undergo a private and public Trial on the Civil Law before the Faculty of Advocates, and be found by them qualified for the said Office, two Years before he be named to be a Lord of the Session: Yet so, as the Qualification made, or to be made, for capacitating Persons to be named ordinary Lords of Session, may be altered by the Parliament of Great-Britain.* And that the Court of Justiciary, do also, after the Union, and notwithstanding thereof, remain, in all time coming within Scotland, as it is now constituted by the laws of

that Kingdom, and with the same Authority and Privileges as before
the Union, subject nevertheless to such Regulations as shall be made
by the Parliament of Great-Britain, and without Prejudice of other
Rights of Justiciary: And that all Admiralty-Jurisdictions be under the
Lord High Admiral, or Commissioners for the Admiralty of Great-
Britain, for the Time being; and that the Court of Admiralty, now
established in Scotland, be continued, and that all Reviews, Reduc-
tions, or Suspensions of the Sentences in Maritime Cases, competent
to the Jurisdiction of that Court, remain in the same Manner after the
Union, as now in Scotland, until the Parliament of Great-Britain
shall make such Regulations and Alterations, as shall be judged
expedient for the whole united Kingdom, so as there be always
continued in Scotland, a Court of Admiralty, such as in England, for
Determination of all Maritime Cases relating to private Rights in
Scotland, competent to the Jurisdiction of the Admiralty Court,
subject nevertheless to such Regulations and Alterations, as shall be
thought proper to be made by the Parliament of Great-Britain; and
that the heritable Rights of Admiralty and Vice-admiralties in Scotland, be reserved to the respective Proprietors, as Rights of Property;
subject nevertheless, as to the Manner of exercising such heritable
Rights, to such Regulations and Alterations, as shall be thought
proper to be made by the Parliament of Great Britain; and that all
other Courts now in being within the Kingdom of Scotland, do
remain, but subject to Alterations by the Parliament of Great-Britain;
and that all inferior Courts, within the said Limits, do remain
subordinate, as they are now, to the supreme Courts of Justice within
the same in all Time coming; and that no Causes in Scotland be
cognizable by the Courts of Chancery, Queen's-Bench, Common-
Pleas, or any other Court in Westminster-Hall; and that the said
Courts, or any other of the like Nature, after the Union, shall have no
Power to cognize, review, or alter the Acts or Sentences of the
Judicatures within Scotland, to stop the Execution of the same. And
that there be a Court of Exchequer in Scotland, after the Union, for
deciding Questions, concerning the Revenues of Customs and Excises
there, having the same Power and Authority in such Cases, as the
Court of Exchequer has in England; and that the said Court of
Exchequer in Scotland have Power of passing Signatures, Gifts,

Tutories, and in other Things, as the Court of Exchequer at present in Scotland hath; and that the Court of Exchequer that now is in Scotland, do remain until a new Court of Exchequer be settled by the Parliament of Great-Britain, in Scotland, after the Union; and that, after the Union, the Queen's Majesty, and her Royal Successors, may continue a Privy-Council in Scotland, for preserving the public Peace and Order, until the Parliament of Great Britain shall think fit to alter it, or establish any other effectual Method for that End.

XX   That all heritable Offices, Superiorities, heritable Jurisdictions, Offices for Life, and Jurisdictions for Life, be reserved for the Owners thereof, as Rights of Property, in the same Manner as they are now enjoyed by the Laws of Scotland, notwithstanding this Treaty.

XXI   That the Rights and Privileges of the Royal Boroughs in Scotland as they are, do remain entire after the Union, and notwithstanding thereof.

XXII   That by Virtue of this Treaty, of the Peers of Scotland, at the Time of the Union, sixteen shall be the Number to sit and vote in the House of Lords, and forty-five the Number of the Representatives of Scotland in the House of Commons of the Parliament of Great Britain; and that, when her Majesty, her Heirs, or Successors, shall declare her or their Pleasure, for holding the first or any subsequent Parliament of Great-Britain, until the Parliament of Great-Britain shall make further Provision therein, a Writ do issue under the Great Seal of the united Kingdom, directed to the Privy-Council of Scotland, commanding them to cause sixteen Peers, who are to sit in the House of Lords, to be summoned to Parliament, and forty-five Members to be elected to sit in the House of Commons in the Parliament of Great-Britain, according to the Agreement in this Treaty, in such Manner as by *an Act of this present Session of* the Parliament of Scotland, is, or shall be settled; *Which Act is hereby declared to be as valid as if it were a Part of, and engrossed in this Treaty.* And that the Names of the Persons so summoned and elected, shall be returned by the Privy-Council of Scotland, into the Court from whence the said Writ did issue. And that, if her Majesty, on or before the first Day of May next, on which Day the Union is to take place, shall declare under the Great Seal of England, that it is expedient,

that the Lords of Parliament of England, and Commons of the
present Parliament of England, should be the Members of the
respective Houses of the first Parliament of Great-Britain, for, and on
the Part of England, then the said Lords of Parliament of England,
and Commons of the present Parliament of England, shall be the
Members of the respective Houses of the first Parliament of Great-
Britain, for, and on the Part of England. And her Majesty may, by her
Royal Proclamation, under the Great Seal of Great-Britain, appoint
the said first Parliament of Great-Britain, to meet at such Time and
Place as her Majesty shall think fit, which Time shall not be less than
fifty Days after the Date of such Proclamation, and the Time and
Place of the Meeting of such Parliament being so appointed, a Writ
shall be immediately issued under the Great Seal of Great-Britain,
directed to the Privy-Council of Scotland for the summoning the
sixteen Peers, and for electing forty-five Members, by whom Scotland
is to be represented in the Parliament of Great-Britain: And the
Lords of Parliament of England, and the sixteen Peers of Scotland,
such sixteen Peers being summoned and returned in the Manner
agreed in this Treaty; and the Members of the House of Commons of
the said Parliament of England, and the forty-five Members for
Scotland, such forty-five Members being elected, and returned in the
Manner agreed in this Treaty, shall assemble and meet respectively,
in their respective Houses of the Parliament of Great-Britain, at such
Time and Place as shall be so appointed by her Majesty, and shall be
the Houses of the first Parliament of Great-Britain, and that Parliament may continue for such Time only as the present Parliament of
England might have continued, if the Union of the two Kingdoms
had not been made, unless sooner dissolved by her Majesty: And that
every one of the Lords of Parliament of Great Britain, and every
Member of the House of Commons of the Parliament of Great-
Britain, in the first, and all succeeding Parliaments of Great-Britain,
until the Parliament of Great-Britain shall otherways direct, shall
take the respective Oaths of Allegiance and Supremacy, by an Act of
Parliament made in England, in the first Year of the Reign of the late
King William and Queen Mary, entitled, *An Act for the abrogating of the
Oaths of Supremacy and Allegiance, and appointing other Oaths,* and make,
subscribe, and audibly repeat the Declaration mentioned in an Act of

Parliament made in England, in the thirtieth Year of the Reign of King Charles the Second, entitled, *An Act for the more effectual preserving the King's Person and Government, by disabling Papists from sitting in either House of Parliament*, and shall take and subscribe the Oath mentioned in an Act of Parliament made in England, in the first Year of her Majesty's Reign, entitled, *An Act to declare the Alterations in the Oath appointed to be taken by the Act*, entitled, *An Act for the further Security of his Majesty's Person, and the Succession of the Crown in the Protestant Line, and for extinguishing the Hopes of the pretended Prince of* Wales, *and all other Pretenders, and their open and secret Abettors, and for the declaring the Association, to be determined at such Time, and in such Manner, as the Members of both Houses of Parliament of England, are by the said respective Acts, directed to take, make and subscribe the same, upon the Penalties and Disabilities in the said respective Acts contained.* And it is declared and agreed, that these Words, this Realm, the Crown of this Realm, and the Queen of this Realm, mentioned in the Oaths and Declaration contained in the aforesaid Acts, which were intended to signify the Crown and Realm of England, shall be understood of the Crown and Realm of Great-Britain; and that in that Sense, the said Oaths and Declaration be taken and subscribed by the Members of both Houses of the Parliament of Great-Britain.

XXIII   That in the aforesaid sixteen Peers of Scotland, mentioned in the last preceeding Article, to sit in the House of Lords of the Parliament of Great-Britain, shall have all Privileges of Parliament, which the Peers of England now have, and which they, or any Peers of Great-Britain, shall have after the Union; and particularly the Right of sitting upon the Tryals of Peers: And, in case of the Tryal of any Peer in time of Adjournment or Prorogation of Parliament, the said sixteen Peers shall be summoned in the same Manner, and have the same Powers and Privileges at such Tryals, as any other Peers of Great-Britain: And that, in case any Tryals of Peers shall hereafter happen, when there is no Parliament in being, the sixteen Peers of Scotland, who sat in the last preceding Parliament, shall be summoned in the same Manner, and have the same Powers and Privileges at such Tryals, as any other Peers of Great-Britain, and that all Peers of Scotland, and their Successors to their Honours and Dignities, shall, from, and after the Union, be Peers of Great-Britain, and have

Rank and Precedency next, and immediately after the Peers of the like Orders and Degrees in England at the Time of the Union, and before all Peers of Great-Britain, of the like Orders and Degrees, who may be created after the Union, and shall be tried as Peers of Great Britain, and shall enjoy all Privileges of Peers as fully as the Peers of England do now, or as they or any other Peers of Great-Britain may hereafter enjoy the same, except the Right and Privilege of sitting in the House of Lords, and the Privileges depending thereon, and particularly the right of sitting upon the Tryals of Peers.

XXIV   That, from and after the Union, there be one Great Seal for the united Kingdom of Great Britain, which shall be different from the Great Seal now used in either Kingdom; and that the quartering the Arms, *and the Rank and Precedency of Lyon King of Arms of the Kingdom of Scotland*, as may best suit the Union, be left to her Majesty: And that, in the mean Time, the Great Seal of England be used as the Great Seal of the united Kingdom, sealing Writs to elect and summon the Parliament of Great-Britain, and for sealing all Treaties with foreign Princes and States, and all public Acts, Instruments, and Orders of State, which concern the whole united Kingdom, and in all other Matters relating to England, as the Great Seal of England is now used; and that a Seal in Scotland, after the Union, be always kept, and made use of in all Things relating to private Rights or Grants, which have usually passed the Great Seal of Scotland, and which only concern Offices, Grants, Commissions, and private Rights within that Kingdom: And that, until such Seal shall be appointed by her Majesty, the present Great-Seal of Scotland shall be used for such Purposes: And that the Privy Seal, Signet-Casset, Signet of the Justiciary Court, Quarter-Seal, and Seals of Courts now used in Scotland, be continued: But that the said Seals be altered and adapted to the State of the Union, as her Majesty shall think fit; and the said Seals, and all of them, and the Keepers of them, shall be subject to such Alterations as the Parliament of Great-Britain shall hereafter make: *And that the Crown, Scepter, and Sword of State, the Records of Parliament, and all other Records, Rolls and Registers whatsoever, both public and private, general and particular, and Warrants thereof, continue to be kept as they are, within that Part of the united Kingdom now called Scotland; and that they shall so remain in all Time coming, notwithstanding of the Union.*

XXV   That all Laws and Statutes in either Kingdom, so far as they are contrary to, or inconsistent with the Terms of these Articles, or any of them, shall, from and after the Union, cease, and become void, and shall be so declared to be, by the respective Parliaments of the said Kingdoms.

SOURCE: *History and Proceedings of the House of Commons,* IV 1742, London, 16–30.

SELECT BIBLIOGRAPHY

Key Printed Primary Sources

Clerk, Sir John, *History of the Union of Scotland and England* (Edinburgh, 1993)

Correspondence of George Baillie of Jerviswoode (Bannatyne Club, Edinburgh, 1828)

Healey, G. H. (ed.), *The Letters of Daniel Defoe* (Oxford, 1955)

Lockhart, G., *Memoirs Concerning the Affairs of Scotland from Queen Anne's Accession to the Commencement of the Union of the Two Kingdoms of Scotland and England in May, 1707* (London, 1714)

Reports on the Manuscripts of the Earl of Mar and Kellie (Historical Manuscripts Commission, London, 1904)

Robertson, J. (ed.), *Andrew Fletcher: Political Works* (Cambridge, 1997)

Articles

Elliot., J. H., 'A Europe of composite monarchies', *Past & Present*, 137 (November 1992), 48–71.

Ferguson, W., 'The Making of the Treaty of Union of 1707', *Scottish Historical Review*, XLIII, 136 (October 1964), 89–110.

Kidd, C., 'North Britishness and the nature of eighteenth-century British patriotisms', *The Historical Journal*, 39, 2 (1996), 361–82.

Macinnes, A. I., 'Studying the Scottish Estates and the Treaty of Union', *History Microcomputer Review*, 6, 2 (Fall 1990), 11–25.

Smout, T. C., 'The Anglo-Scottish Union of 1707, I. The Economic background', *Economic History Review*, XVI, 1–3 (1963–4), 455–67.

Whatley, C. A., 'Economic causes and Consequences of the Union of 1707: A Survey', *Scottish Historical Review*, LXVIII, 186 (October 1989), 150–81.

Books and Edited Collections

Bradshaw, B. and Morrill, J. (eds.), *The British Problem, c.1534–1707: State Formation in the Atlantic Archipelago* (Basingstoke, 1996).

Connolly, S. J. (ed.), *Kingdoms United? Great Britain and Ireland since 1500* (Dublin, 1999).

Dicey, A. V. and Rait, R. S., *Thoughts on the Union between England and Scotland* (London, 1920).

Ellis, S. G. and Barber, S., *Conquest & Union: Fashioning a British State, 1485–1725* (London, 1995).

Ferguson, W., *Scotland's Relations with England: A Survey to 1707* (Edinburgh, 1994 ed.).

Goodare, J., *State and Society in Early Modern Scotland* (Oxford, 1999).

Holmes, G. (ed.), *Britain After the Glorious Revolution, 1689–1714* (London, 1969).

Kidd, C., *Subverting Scotland's Past: Scottish Whig Historians and the Creation of an Anglo-British Identity, 1689–c.1830* (Cambridge, 1993).

MacKinnon, J., *The Union of England and Scotland: A Study in International History* (London, 1896).

Riley, P. W. J., *The Union of England and Scotland: A Study in Anglo-Scottish Politics of the Eighteenth Century* (Manchester, 1978).

Robertson, J (ed.), *A Union for Empire: Political Thought and the Union of 1707* (Cambridge, 1995).

Scott, P. H., *Andrew Fletcher and the Treaty of Union* (Edinburgh, 1992).

Scott, P. H., *'The Boasted Advantages': The Consequences of the Union of 1707* (Edinburgh, 1999).

Smith, D. L., *A History of the Modern British Isles, 1603–1707: The Double Crown* (Oxford, 1998).

Smout, T. C., *Scottish Trade on the Eve of Union, 1660–1707* (Edinburgh, 1963).

Whatley, C. A., *Scottish Society, 1707–1830: Beyond Jacobitism, Towards Industrialisation* (Manchester, 2000).

INDEX